Easy Latin

Puzzles

Julian Morgan

DEDICATION

This book is dedicated to the memory of a wonderful teacher,
without whose shared knowledge and enthusiasm
my world would have been a very different place.

James H Eggleshaw

ACKNOWLEDGEMENTS

Thanks go to my old friend Mark Ranshaw for staying up very late one night with me to work on the front cover. Thanks also to the eagle-eyed Evita Müller.

CONTENTS

Introduction

Easy Latin Puzzles?

Should that mean easy Latin, easy puzzles, or both?

Well as far as the Latin goes, this book uses a set of vocabulary commonly featured in different study books, so it should be accessible to most students in their early stages as well as to adults whose recollections from their quondam days may be a little hazy. Not only that, this book does not make use of endings systems, so you won't need to worry about tricky inflections as you work through the puzzles. On top of all that and for those of you who get stuck, the answers are all in the back!

So much for the easy Latin then. As to whether the puzzles themselves should be called easy, that will be for you to decide along your way. There are three levels and you can find all of the words used for each of these at the back of the book. That may help but as you work your way through your challenges, perhaps you should expect them to get more difficult.

Quizzes 1 to 17 are based on Word List 1 (208 words)
Quizzes 18 to 34 are based on Word List 2 (208 words)
Quizzes 35 to 47 are based on Word List 3 (195 words)

Quizzes 48 to 60 are based on all three lists, as well as a few extra words which you will find in Word List 4 (38 words).

This new edition of the book has been significantly improved and added to from the previous one, though the concept itself has not changed. Several puzzles have been replaced or tweaked and there are ten completely new ones included here too.

Good luck with the puzzles and please email me if you see ways by which I can improve this book or if you have have ideas about other new projects.

julian@j-progs.com

1   Mini crossword

The clues are in Latin but the answers are in English. If you need help, refer to Word List 1 at the back of the book.

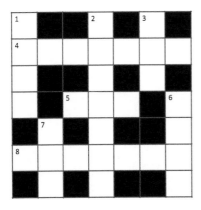

Across

4.   Miles (7)
5.   Rogo (3)
8.   Cubiculum (7)

Down

1.   Dico (1,3)
2.   Cupio (1,6)
3.   Video (3)
6.   Domus (4)
7.   Novus (3)

*Note: where a verb is the clue, such as **iaceo - I lie**, the word **I** may be omitted or included in your answer.*

2   Latin mini

The clues are in English but the answers are in Latin. If you need help, refer to Word List 1 at the back of the book.

Across

1.   Why (3)
2.   I do (3)
3.   New (5)
6.   However (5)
7.   Her (3)
8.   Voice (3)

Down

1.   Dog (5)
2.   I am absent (5)
4.   Prayer (5)
5.   Old man (5)

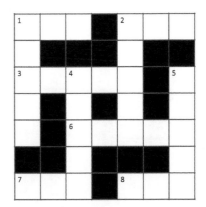

3   He's the boss

Fill in the words going across and you will discover a Roman boss, once you can read the word going down on the left side of the grid. His name, by the way, is given here in Latin. If you need help, refer to Word List 1 at the back of the book.

Clues

1.	Anger	
2.	Where	
3.	Through	
4.	Foot	
5.	There	
6.	Then	
7.	I	
8.	King	

The boss is: ....

4   The lonely soldier

In the table below, the words have all been taken out and printed underneath, all except one – MILES, which means soldier. Your job is to fit all the other words back into the grid.

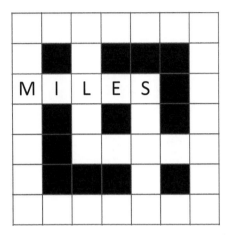

5 Letters

MALUS

~~MILES~~

SEDEO

SED IN

7 Letters

DOMINUS

DIMITTO

STO ROGO

OSTENDO

5   A happy task

*Look carefully at the grid below. The object of the puzzle is to find out which letter of the alphabet is represented by each of the 13 numbers used. You are given one word to start you off, so you can begin by entering any letters from this word wherever they appear in the grid. Each word you make should be in good Latin (you can check Word List 1 if you need to). As you decode each letter, write it in the **Letters deciphered** table and cross it off in the **Letters used** table.*

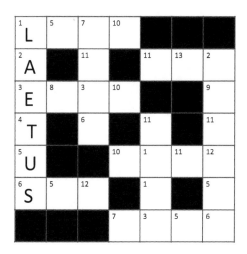

Letters deciphered

1	2	3	4	5	6	7	8	9	10	11	12	13
L	A	E	T	U	S							

Letters used

A D E̶ I L̶ M N O R S̶ T̶ U̶ X

5

6   Roman Emperors

See how many Roman emperors you can find in the grid. A whole bunch of them have been listed below and then hidden in the grid: your job is to find them. Words may go across, backwards, up, down or diagonally.

A	U	G	U	S	T	U	S	N	A	N	V	L	E	R	I	V	C
N	S	E	V	E	R	U	S	A	L	E	X	A	N	D	E	R	O
T	S	S	R	E	D	S	U	N	A	J	A	R	T	I	P	R	M
O	B	V	D	H	F	C	E	A	L	C	G	V	Q	O	R	U	M
N	S	V	M	H	A	L	U	G	I	L	A	C	M	C	T	D	O
I	U	V	R	A	N	A	I	T	I	M	O	D	B	L	M	T	D
N	I	E	C	D	N	O	D	R	N	N	T	C	H	E	V	K	U
U	L	S	U	R	E	V	E	S	S	U	I	M	I	T	P	E	S
S	E	P	R	I	R	O	C	T	V	U	T	G	L	I	G	R	L
P	R	A	R	A	O	O	A	N	B	Q	U	M	H	A	X	M	N
I	U	S	R	N	A	N	S	Q	A	L	S	A	K	N	F	G	A
U	A	I	Q	A	T	G	U	S	U	I	R	E	B	I	T	T	I
S	S	A	L	I	E	B	I	R	T	S	L	G	T	B	A	P	R
T	U	N	N	R	G	E	D	N	M	Q	I	E	U	V	A	D	E
C	C	E	T	R	M	N	U	G	R	O	X	S	R	G	T	X	L
E	R	F	K	A	B	L	A	G	T	F	B	E	B	U	Q	G	A
R	A	V	I	T	E	L	L	I	U	S	N	I	Z	T	A	S	V
I	M	Z	C	A	R	A	C	A	L	L	A	G	U	O	H	T	O

ANTONINUS PIUS	DIOCLETIAN	OTHO
AUGUSTUS	DOMITIAN	SEPTIMIUS SEVERUS
AURELIAN	GALBA	SEVERUS ALEXANDER
CALIGULA	GETA	TIBERIUS
CARACALLA	HADRIAN	TITUS
CLAUDIUS	MARCUS AURELIUS	TRAJAN
COMMODUS	NERO	VALERIAN
CONSTANTINE	NERVA	VESPASIAN
		VITELLIUS

7   Sudoku

You know how Sudoku works. All you have to do is to place numbers one to nine in each vertical and horizontal line and then make sure that each number appears once in each of the nine 3x3 squares. The difference here is that this is Roman Sudoku! In this challenge, you use the numbers as below.

Roman numbers

1	2	3	4	5	6	7	8	9
I	II	III	IV	V	VI	VII	VIII	IX

Good luck – prosit!

III		IV		VII	VIII		VI	
					I	II	IX	
I	VI				IV			III
II					IX	III	I	
		VIII	V		VI	IX		
	V	III	I					VII
IV			VI				V	VIII
	VII	V	VIII					
	IX		IV	II		VII		VI

8   Crossword

The clues are in Latin but the answers are in English. If you need help, refer to Word List 1 at the back of the book.

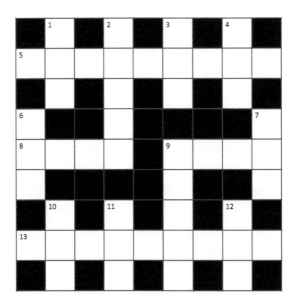

Across

5. Strenuus (9)
8. Olim (4)
9. Gero (4)
13. Nuntius (9)

Down

1. Et (3)
2. Fortis (5)
3. Video (3)
4. Fragor (3)
6. Quam (3)
7. Lacrimo (3)
9. Vulnus (5)
10. Conspicio (3)
11. Quaero (3)
12. Novus (3)

*Note: where a verb is the clue, such as **iaceo - I lie**, the word **I** may be omitted or included in your answer.*

9   Beware of the dog!

A fierce dog is stopping you from getting in the house. If you know his name, you will be able to call him off. Fill in the grid and work out who he is by putting together the letters in the shaded boxes. Use Word List 1 for help.

<u>Across</u>
1. Often (5)
4. Centurion (8)
8. I go down (8)
11. I go away (4)
12. I give (2)
13. She (4)
15. Them (3)
16. I buy (3)
17. While (3)
18. You (plural) (3)
19. I push back (7)

23. Him (3)
26. I fall (4)
27. I tell (5)
28. Huge (6)

<u>Down</u>
2. From (2)
3. Poet (5)
5. City (4)
6. I lie (5)
7. Says (6)

9. Sky (6)
10. I owe (5)
12. Home (5)
14. I arrive (7)
15. Out of (2)
18. Neighbouring (7)
20. I leave (4)
21. I do (5)
22. Because (4)
24. Mountain (4)
25. Was (4)

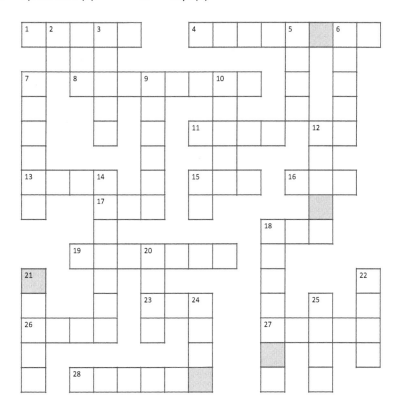

The dog's name is: ....

10   Crossword

The clues are in English but the answers are in Latin. If you need help, refer to Word List 1 at the back of the book.

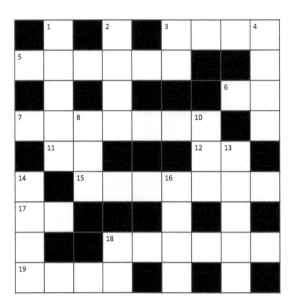

Across

3. To be (4)
5. Soon night (3,3)
6. My (2)
7. Day, but (4,3)
11. You are (2)
12. He (2)
15. Then, boy (3,4)
17. There (2)
18. At last (6)
19. Alas (4)

Down

1. Today (5)
2. One (4)
3. Out of (2)
4. Leaves (4)
8. Is (3)
10. For a long time (3)
13. I sit (5)
14. Well (4)
16. I put (4)
18. You (singular) (2)

11 Cryptic Latin crossword

The answers to this mind-bender are all in Latin. You may need to use Word List 1 for help.

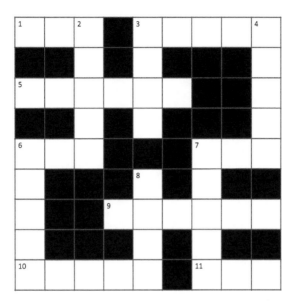

Across

1. This chap sounds rather tipsy, perhaps (3)
3. Mixed up grouse loses direction and rises up (5)
5. Room in a triumphant hall (6)
6. I need money for this but not in New York (3)
7. Road from a mixed up six (3)
9. There's none to annul lust in there (6)
10. Dish up on the brakes (5)
11. I just love the first conjugation (3)

Down

2. I'm not walking (5)
3. His or hers - sounds like dirty business (4)
4. Insomnia without sin affects everything (5)
6. Cavalryman's essential equipment (5)
7. A place to live's fifty-fifty in the road (5)
8. No learner could take first place (4)

12   Arrowword

All the clues are on the grid. You can use Word List 1 at the back to help if you want. The answers should all be in Latin.

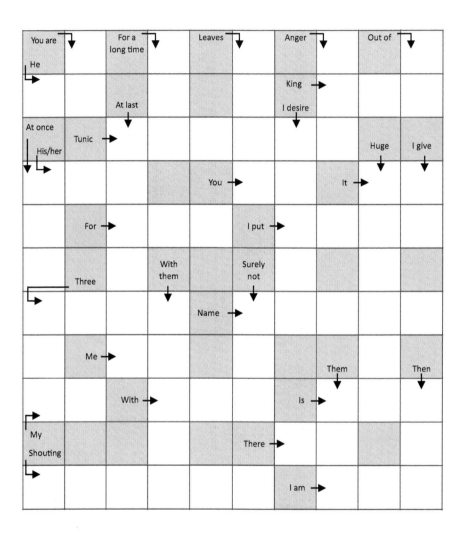

13   A great man

Fill in the words in Latin going across and then you will discover a great Roman, once you can read the word which goes down through the middle of the grid. Use Word List 1 for help.

Clues

1.	Danger (9)
2.	Human (4)
3.	Money (7)
4.	I climb (7)
5.	Bravely (8)
6.	Wood (5)
7.	Door (5)
8.	I send (5)
9.	I hear (5)
10.	Woman (6)
11.	I wait for (8)

The great man is: ....

14   It's your game

In the table below, the words have been taken out and printed underneath. Your job is to fit them all back into the grid. Your starting point should be obvious: the clue is in the title of this puzzle.

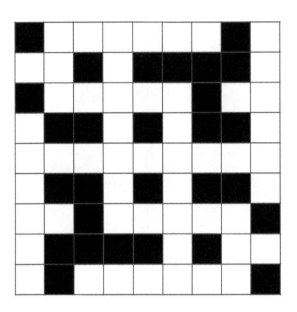

2 Letters	**6 Letters**
EX	EXCITO
IS	IBI EST
ME	ILLE ES
SI	LABORO

3 Letters	**7 Letters**
AMO	CONSUMO
EST	OSTENDO

5 Letters	**9 Letters**
OMNIA	LUDUS TUUS
TENEO	

15   Latin crossword

The clues are in English but the answers are all in Latin. If you need help, refer to Word List 1 at the back of the book.

Across

4. God (4)
6. Centurion (8)
8. Name (5)
9. I fight (5)
11. Soldier (5)
13. For a long time if (3,2)
14. I turn (5)
15. Sad (5)
19. Your, her (4,4)
20. Alas (4)

Down

1. Fiercely (9)
2. And me (2,2)
3. In front of (3)
4. I give (2)
5. Himself (2)
7. One with them (4,5)
10. Where (3)
12. Is (3)
16. Herself (4)
17. Why (3)
18. You (2)
19. You (singular) (2)

16   Crossword

The clues are in Latin but the answers are all in English. If you need help, refer to Word List 1 at the back of the book.

Across

1. Trado (4,4)
5. Ingens (4)
7. Saepe (5)
10. Sum (2)
11. Sed (3)
12. Verbero (1,4)
13. Saluto (5)
14. Sunt (3)
15. In (2)
16. Hodie (5)
17. Toga (4)
20. Subito (8)

Down

2. Cinis (3)
3. Canis (3)
4. Diu (4,4)
6. Consumo id (3,2)
8. Ibi (5)
9. Filia (8)
11. Panis (5)
12. Volo (1,4)
18. Debeo (3)
19. Omnis (3)

*Note: where a verb is the clue, such as **iaceo - I lie**, the word **I** may be omitted or included in your answer.*

17   Action speaks

Find the Latin verbs which have been listed below and then hidden in the grid. They may be written across or down, or even diagonally. Oh yes, they could even be written backwards!

B	D	O	I	N	V	E	N	I	O	Q	U	I	E	S	C	O	O
O	I	G	U	F	F	T	A	C	E	O	V	U	O	T	C	R	O
R	S	B	P	O	R	T	R	O	I	N	E	V	N	O	C	O	R
I	C	R	O	G	E	L	E	N	O	N	N	O	M	O	L	H	T
U	E	B	R	E	D	E	O	A	R	O	I	N	N	T	A	P	N
B	D	H	T	E	D	T	O	C	R	F	O	V	I	B	M	A	I
E	O	A	O	O	E	N	C	E	N	O	R	I	T	O	R	H
O	O	B	O	E	O	N	T	I	N	C	R	T	P	E	T	O	C
T	F	E	D	D	R	E	I	P	O	R	O	N	G	U	P	S	O
C	E	O	E	I	R	O	N	I	P	R	O	M	I	T	T	O	Q
U	S	O	C	R	D	E	C	O	T	C	O	V	E	R	T	O	U
R	T	S	O	C	O	N	I	C	I	O	T	C	E	P	S	S	O
O	I	M	R	O	D	P	T	R	O	N	I	O	R	O	B	A	L
T	N	R	P	R	A	S	O	R	D	T	S	C	R	I	B	O	U
G	O	A	S	C	E	N	D	O	A	E	X	C	I	T	O	O	B
O	M	E	G	A	U	D	E	O	R	N	S	T	O	C	T	C	M
P	L	A	U	D	O	E	M	I	T	D	V	V	O	C	O	I	A
O	B	O	E	O	E	V	A	C	B	O	E	N	A	M	R	D	B

ACCIPIO	CONVENIO	GAUDEO	LEGO	RIDEO
AMBULO	CONVOCO	GEMO	MANEO	SCRIBO
ASCENDO	COQUO	HABEO	PARO	SPECTO
BIBO	CURO	HABITO	PETO	TACEO
CADO	DICO	INCITO	PORTO	TENEO
CAPIO	DISCEDO	INTRO	PROCEDO	TIMEO
CAVEO	DORMIO	INVENIO	PROMITTO	TRADO
CENO	ERRO	IUBEO	PUGNO	VENIO
CLAMO	EXCITO	IUVO	QUIESCO	VERTO
CONICIO	FESTINO	LABORO	REDDO	VOCO
CONTENDO	FUGIO	LAUDO	REDEO	

18   Mini crossword

The clues are in Latin but the answers are in English. If you need help, refer to Word List 2 at the back of the book.

Across

1. Dea (7)
4. Non (3)
6. Bos (3)
7. Aura (3)
8. Doctus (7)

Down

1. Imperator (7)
2. Fossa (5)
3. Tam fessus (2,5)
5. Moneo (1,4)

*Note: where a verb is the clue, such as **iaceo - I lie**, the word **I** may be omitted or included in your answer.*

19   Latin mini

The clues are in English but the answers are in Latin. If you need help, refer to Word List 2 at the back of the book.

Across

1. Unknown (7)
5. I attend (7)
6. About form (2,5)

Down

2. I taste (5)
3. I observe (7)
4. I am present (5)

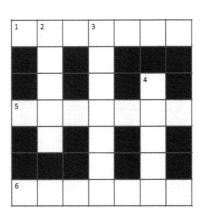

20   What do you mean?

Fill in the words going across and then you will uncover a Latin expression going down through the middle of the grid, which is commonly used in English. Word List 2 should help you find the right answers if you get stuck.

Clues

1.   I prevent (7)

2.   Scarcely (3)

3.   I understand (9)

4.   I order (6)

5.   I overcome (6)

6.   Slowly (5)

7.   I snatch (5)

8.   Master (8)

9.   In vain (7)

10.   Hello (5)

11.   Couch (6)

12.   Then (6)

13   Other (5)

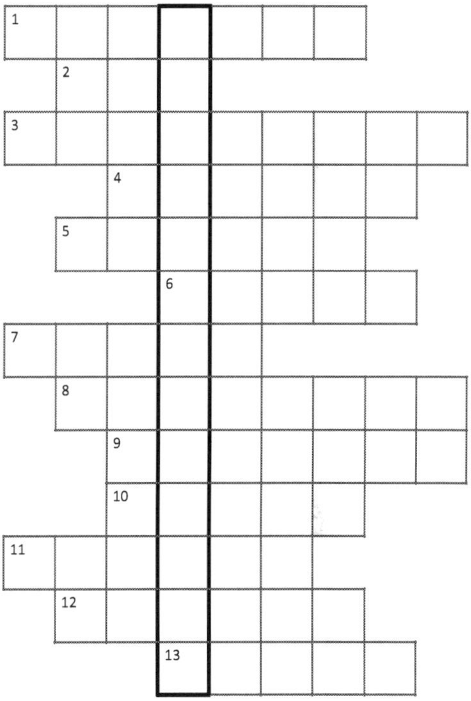

The expression is: ....

21   The abandoned flower

In the table below, the words have been taken out and printed underneath, all except one – FLOS, which means flower. Your job is to fit all the other words back into the grid.

4 Letters	7 Letters
AMOR	EFFUGIO
CRAS	EXTRAHO
MEUS	OPTIMUS
~~FLOS~~	RECUMBO
NOLO	
NUNC	
ROTA	
SCIO	

22   I recognise that!

*Look carefully at the grid below. The object of the puzzle is to find out which letter of the alphabet is represented by each of the 17 numbers used. You are given one word to start you off, so you can begin by entering any letters from this word wherever they appear in the grid. Each word you make should be in good Latin (you can check Word List 2 if you need to). As you decode each letter, write it in the **Letters deciphered** table and cross it off among the **Letters used**.*

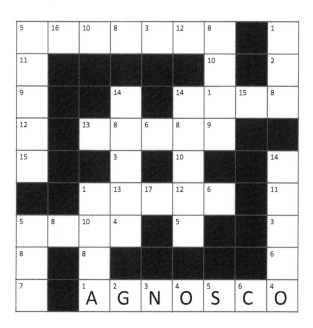

Letters deciphered

1	2	3	4	5	6	7	8	9	10	11	12	13	14	15	16	17
A	G	N	O	S	C											

Letters used

A ~~C~~ D E ~~G~~ H I L M ~~N~~ ~~O~~ R ~~S~~ T U V X

23   Roman gods

See how many Roman gods you can find in the grid below. Their names may be written across or down, or even diagonally. Oh yes, they could also be written backwards!

S	M	D	I	A	N	A	U	T	A	S	C	S	P	S
E	I	S	F	V	A	P	O	L	L	O	U	I	O	R
L	N	O	A	U	T	S	J	U	N	O	P	P	O	E
U	E	N	U	L	B	P	L	U	T	O	I	A	S	T
C	R	E	N	C	A	S	U	D	E	M	D	R	D	I
R	V	P	U	A	M	I	T	H	R	A	S	E	P	P
E	A	T	S	N	B	C	U	P	I	R	L	S	R	U
H	Y	U	T	L	Y	A	D	P	T	S	C	O	O	J
S	R	N	P	N	R	U	T	A	S	A	Y	T	S	B
B	U	E	C	L	I	S	I	S	S	R	B	E	E	A
P	C	R	M	M	T	S	E	R	E	C	E	L	R	C
E	R	O	V	E	N	U	S	M	P	V	G	E	P	C
A	E	R	A	R	R	S	J	A	N	U	S	B	I	H
O	M	A	F	O	R	T	U	N	A	L	T	Y	N	U
A	E	S	C	U	L	A	P	I	U	S	T	C	A	S

AESCULAPIUS	HERCULES	MITHRAS
APOLLO	ISIS	NEPTUNE
BACCHUS	JANUS	PLUTO
CERES	JUNO	PROSERPINA
CUPID	JUPITER	SATURN
CYBELE	MARS	SERAPIS
DIANA	MEDUSA	VENUS
FAUNUS	MERCURY	VESTA
FORTUNA	MINERVA	VULCAN

24   Sudoku

You know how Sudoku works. All you have to do is to place numbers one to nine in each vertical and horizontal line and then make sure that each number appears once in each of the nine 3x3 squares. The difference here is that this is Roman Sudoku! In this challenge, you use the numbers as below.

Roman numbers

1	2	3	4	5	6	7	8	9
I	II	III	IV	V	VI	VII	VIII	IX

Good luck – prosit!

VII				III	VIII		V	
VI			I	VII		IX	III	
	III	IX			II			
III	I			II		VIII		VI
VIII		IV	III		VII	I		V
II				IX			VII	
			IV			III	VIII	
	VIII	V		I				IX
	VII		II	VIII				I

25   Latin crossword

The clues are in English but the answers are all in Latin. If you need help, refer to Word List 2 at the back of the book.

Across

2. Camp (6)
4. I cleanse (5)
6. Again (6)
8. I do not want (4)
10. Wine (5)
11. Love (4)
12. Greedy (6)
14. Shadow (5)
15. At first (6)

Down

1. Field (4)
3. Sign (6)
5. Flower (4)
7. Table (5)
9. Fame (4)
10. Word (6)
13. Armour (4)

26 Members of a club

Fill in the grid to discover three members of a well known Roman club. Put together the letters from the shaded boxes to try to make three names from the letters. Use Word List 2 if you need help.

Across

3. I approach (6)
6. Sailor (5)
8. Also (2)
10. Task (4)
11. Peace (3)
12. Garden (6)
13. Who (3)
14. Eight (4)
15. Mouth (2)
16. Scarcely (3)
17. First (6)
18. I kill (4)
20. Six (3)
22. Wax (4)
25. She (2)
26. I put down (6)
27. Between (5)
29. Look (4)
30. On account of (2)
31. Good (4)
32. I bear (4)
33. I was (4)

Down

1. House (4)
2. But (2)
3. I open (6)
4. Two (3)
5. I do not know (6)
7. Up to now (5)
9. Four (8)
11. Dust (6)
13. Five hundred (9)
17. Leader (8)
19. I beg (3)
21. I exercise (7)
23. Hurray (4)
24. I help (6)
28. Rose (4)

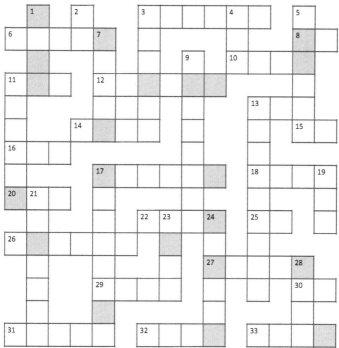

The three club members are:

....

....

....

27   Crossword

The clues are in Latin but the answers are all in English. If you need help, refer to Word List 2 at the back of the book.

Across

6. Circumspecto (1,4,6)
7. Tempto (1,3)
8. Anulus (4)
9. Iterum (5)
10. Mors (5)
12. Id est (2,2)
14. Age (4)
15. Praeterea tantum (7,4)

Down

1. Cuncti (3,8)
2. Tam meus (2,2)
3. Plaustrum (5)
4. Porta (4)
5. Neque parvus (3,3,5)
11. Commotus (5)
13. Navis (4)
14. Coquus (4)

*Note: where a verb is the clue, such as **iaceo - I lie**, the word **I** may be omitted or included in your answer.*

28   Cryptic Latin crossword

The answers to this brain-teaser are all in Latin. You may need to use Word List 2 for help.

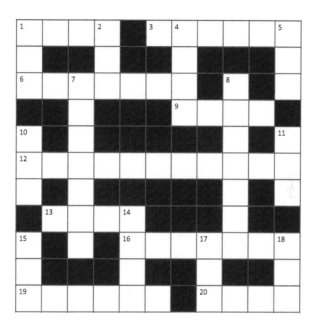

Across

1. Not quite round goes back for a wash (4)
3. Pensioner confused about anger opening (6)
6. Best wrestler upset about tip (7)
9. Such a story on the face of it (4)
12. Status Floyd needs a strut to approach (11)
13. Inquisition about identity (4)
16. I scald you, so hot (7)
19. Improvement of 51 about Rome (6)
18. Top pretence for ten (4)

Down

1. Roars in the apple orchard (3)
2. Zodiac sign's about hate (3)
4. Stop upset after (4)
5. Joey confused and begging (3)
7. Plummet down to holy place (7)
8. Something to drink? (7)
10. Quiet – stop fighting! (3)
11. Looks like a top milker (3)
14. Know so about a hundred and one (4)
15. An abandoned mania already? (3)
17. Such an Italian start (3)
18. Let the parents explain this number (3)

29   Arrowword

All the clues are on the grid. You can use Word List 1 at the back to help if you want. The answers should all be in Latin.

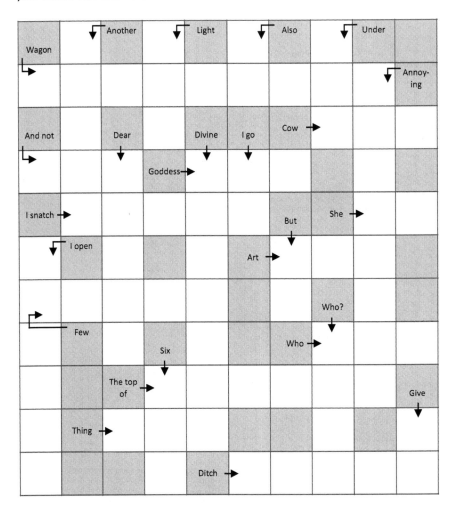

30   Writer's block

Fill in the Latin words going across and you will discover a well known Roman author, when you can read the word which goes down through the middle of the grid. Use Word List 2 for help.

Clues

1.   I take out (7)

2.   Enemy (5)

3.   Part (4)

4.   Fight (5)

5.   I cease (5)

6.   I applaud (6)

7.   Five (7)

8.   Crowd (5)

9.   Spear (5)

10.   Earth (5)

11.   Even (5)

12.   I shine (5)

13.   Farmer (8)

14.   Shore (5)

15   Wave (4)

16   Cloud (5)

The well known Roman author is: ....

31   There's a way

In the table below, the words have been taken out and printed underneath, all except two – ITER, which means a way. Your job is to fit all the other words back into the grid.

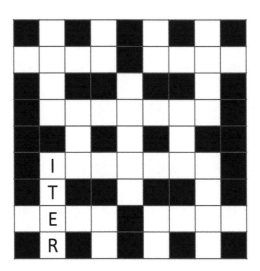

2 Letters	4 Letters	5 Letters
AT	AURA	ALTER
DE	CERA	
EA	CRAS	**7 Letters**
EO	DATE	
	~~ITER~~	IMPEDIO
3 Letters	MEUS	STULTUS
	NEMO	
TAM	OCTO	
UBI		

32   Latin crossword

The clues are in English but the answers are all in Latin. If you need help, refer to Word List 2 at the back of the book.

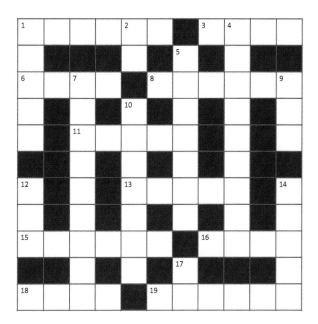

Across		Down	
1.	Brother (6)	1.	Happy (5)
3.	Look (4)	2.	She (2)
6.	I wash (4)	4.	Advice (9)
8.	Sleep (6)	5.	Farmer (7)
11.	I spend winter (5)	7.	Vehicle (9)
13.	Few (5)	9.	Under (3)
15.	Much (6)	10.	Temple (7)
16.	Love (4)	12.	Already (3)
18.	Armour (4)	14.	Fierce (5)
19.	Liar (6)	17.	About (2)

33 Crossword

The clues are in Latin but the answers are all in English. If you need help, refer to Word List 2 at the back of the book.

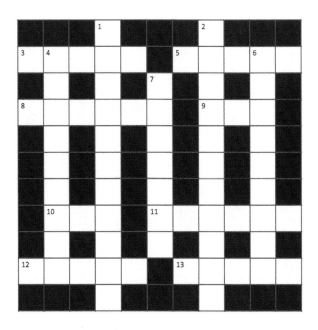

Across

3. Traho (1,4)
5. Quinquaginta (5)
8. Et possum (3,3)
9. Auris (3)
10. Non (3)
11. Tristis aura (3,3)
12. Duo aut (3,2)
13. Paratus (5)

Down

1. Evigilo (5,3,3)
2. Quingenti (4,7)
4. Nescio (2,3,4)
6. Territus (9)
7. Aeternus (7)

*Note: where a verb is the clue, such as **iaceo - I lie**, the word **I** may be omitted or included in your answer.*

34   What are you like?

Find the Latin adjectives in the grid below. They may be written across, down, or even diagonally. Oh yes, they could also be written backwards!

I	N	O	B	I	L	I	S	U	T	O	T	O	P	B	U
G	D	I	F	F	I	C	I	L	I	S	S	C	R	O	T
N	P	R	A	I	C	A	R	U	S	M	I	C	I	N	I
A	L	A	C	N	S	U	U	T	R	O	M	U	M	U	L
V	E	T	I	S	S	U	S	S	E	F	M	P	U	S	I
U	N	U	L	U	U	S	I	S	T	E	O	A	S	U	S
S	U	S	I	T	G	U	S	U	T	R	B	T	S	D	U
U	S	U	S	O	N	S	U	T	I	O	I	U	U	I	C
M	I	T	U	N	O	I	N	A	S	X	L	S	T	G	I
R	N	N	T	G	L	L	I	R	N	T	I	G	I	I	T
I	F	E	L	I	X	A	V	A	R	U	S	A	C	R	S
F	E	T	U	A	N	T	I	P	S	U	U	T	A	F	U
N	L	N	T	I	T	O	D	I	R	A	T	A	T	E	R
I	I	O	S	I	M	U	L	T	U	S	C	A	L	D	E
I	X	C	A	R	N	I	S	S	U	T	S	E	L	O	M
I	N	V	I	T	U	S	U	M	I	T	P	O	R	S	S

AVARUS
BONUS
CARUS
CONTENTUS
DIFFICILIS
DIVINUS
FACILIS
FATUUS
FELIX

FEROX
FESSUS
FRIGIDUS
IGNAVUS
IGNOTUS
IMMOBILIS
INFELIX
INFIRMUS
INVITUS

IRATUS
LATUS
LONGUS
MOLESTUS
MORTUUS
MULTUS
NOBILIS
OCCUPATUS
OPTIMUS

PARATUS
PLENUS
PRIMUS
RUSTICUS
SACER
STULTUS
TACITUS
TALIS
TOTUS
UTILIS

35   Mini crossword

The clues are in Latin but the answers are in English. If you need help, refer to Word List 3 at the back of the book.

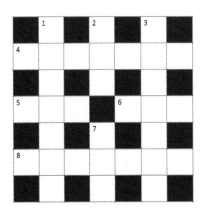

Across

4. Evado (1,6)
5. Filius (3)
6. Taberna (3)
8. Orator in curia (7)

Down

1. Recupero (7)
2. In fabula? (3)
3. Sententia (7)
7. Bellum (3)

*Note: where a verb is the clue, such as **iaceo - I lie**, the word **I** may be omitted or included in your answer.*

36   Latin mini

The clues are in English but the answers are in Latin. If you need help, refer to Word List 3 at the back.

Across

4. From everywhere (7)
5. Man (3)
6. Spring (3)
8. I smell (7)

Down

1. Slave girl (7)
2. Here (3)
3. Young man (7)
7. Them (3)

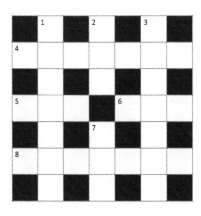

37   All at home

What do all these characters share? Fill in the words going across and you will uncover a Latin word going down. Word List 3 should help you find the right answers if you get stuck.

Clues

1. Father (5)
2. Guest (6)
3. Mistress (6)
4. Doorkeeper (7)
5. Son (6)
6. Young man (7)
7. Slave girl (7)
8. Husband (7)
9. Slave (6)
10. Mother (5)

The characters all share: ....

38   What?

In the table below, the words have been taken out and printed underneath, all except for the word QUID, meaning what. Your job is to fit all the other words back into the grid.

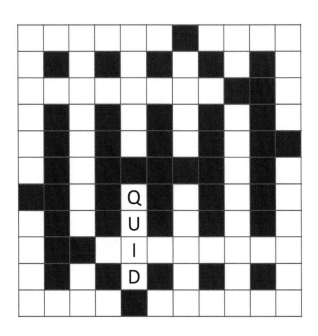

2 Letters

IN
SE

4 Letters

GENS
ORDO
~~QUID~~
SINO
SPES
VEHO

5 Letters

CAPUT
PAENE

6 Letters

CURSUS
DENSUS
IGITUR
INVOCO

8 Letters

ANXIETAS
ISTE PUER
LIBERTUS
VITUPERO

39   A challenge in the arena

*Look carefully at the grid below. The object of the puzzle is to find out which letter of the alphabet is represented by each of the 16 numbers used. You are given one word to start you off, so you can begin by entering any letters from this word wherever they appear in the grid. Each word you make should be in good Latin (you can check Word List 3 if you need to). As you decode each letter, write it in the **Letters deciphered** table and cross it off among the **Letters used**.*

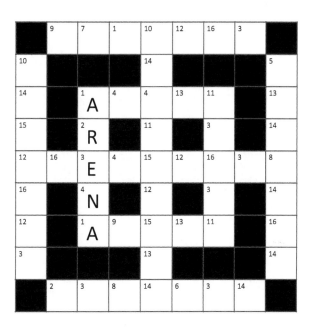

Letters deciphered

1	2	3	4	5	6	7	8	9	10	11	12	13	14	15	16
A	R	E	N												

Letters used

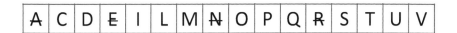

A C D E̶ I L M N̶ O P Q R̶ S T U V

40   Latin crossword

The clues are in English but the answers are all in Latin. If you need help, refer to Word List 3 at the back of the book.

Across

2.   Thus (3)
5.   Palace (4)
7.   I weep (4)
8.   Island (6)
9.   So many (3)
12.   Gift (5)
13.   Citizen (5)
16.   Law (3)
18.   I fall down (6)
20.   I go towards (4)
21.   Only (4)
22.   Altar (3)

Down

1.   Games (4)
3.   I raise (5)
4.   I forbid (4)
6.   Heat (6)
10.   To (2)
11.   Too much (6)
14.   Themselves (2)
15.   Ill (5)
17.   From where (4)
19.   Series (4)

41   A top place

Fill in the grid below to uncover a very important place in Rome. Put together the letters from the shaded boxes and see if you can make one name. Use Word List 3 if you need help.

Across
1. Series (4)
5. I learn (5)
8. I recite (6)
10. Way (3)
12. Merchant (8)
13. I enter (4)
14. I prefer (4)
15. I count (6)
18. Judge (5)
20. School (6)
22. I sing (4)

23. I announce (6)
25. The next day (9)
27. Which (4)
28. Money (3)
29. Greatly (9)

Down
2. Truly (2,4)
3. Speech (6)
4. To him (2)
5. I grieve (5)

6. Themselves (2)
7. Clear (6)
9. Comrade (5)
11. Father (5)
16. Thousand (5)
17. I smell (7)
19. Worthy (6)
21. Delay (4)
23. Recently (5)
24. Life (4)
26. Countryside (3)
27. To where (3)

The top place was: ....

39

42   Crossword

The clues are in Latin but the answers are all in English. If you need help, refer to Word List 3 at the back of the book.

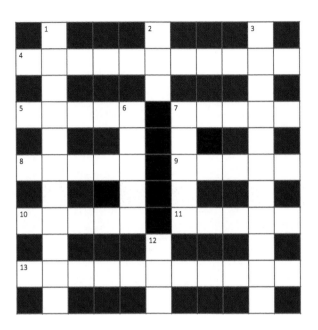

Across

4.   Celerrime (4,7)
5.   Tollo (5)
7.   Hospes (5)
8.   Occupo (5)
9.   Eicio (5)
10. Humilis (5)
11. Tabella (5)
13. Sterto re vera (1,5,5)

Down

1.   Curia (6,5)
2.   Poculum (3)
3.   Claudo placide (5,6)
6.   Inimicus (5)
7.   Magnus (5)
12. Mare (3)

*Note: where a verb is the clue, such as **iaceo - I lie**, the word **I** may be omitted or included in your answer.*

43   Cryptic Latin crossword

The answers to this brain-teaser are all in Latin. You may need to use Word List 3 for help.

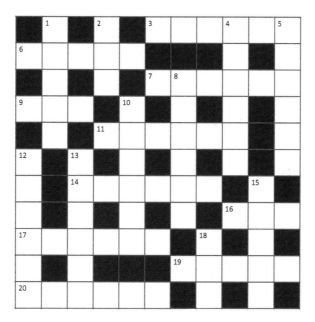

Across

3. Not mum's country? (6)
6. Keep tight-lipped with us on the ground (5)
7. Sweet peck on the cheek sounds rather boring (6)
9. Rodent counts backwards (3)
11. 100 lines upset protegée (6)
14. Hole in the roof's an eyeful (6)
16. Thief in furious rage (3)
17. Spartacus tosses guard inside (6)
19. Cut is just as expected (5)
20. Woman appears more stubborn (6)

Down

1. Rum use of a wall with no direction (5)
2. No idea where status has got to (3)
4. Cures love rejection (6)
5. Sue sat confused in the heat (6)
8. Take responsibility for body part (6)
10. Praise company outside for closure (6)
12. It's around about that (6)
13. Cheating Sulla's lead wins double top (6)
15. Peter's large canine, perhaps? (5)
18. Become upset if zero (3)

44   Arrowword

All the clues are on the grid. You can use Word List 3 at the back to help if you want. The answers should all be in Latin.

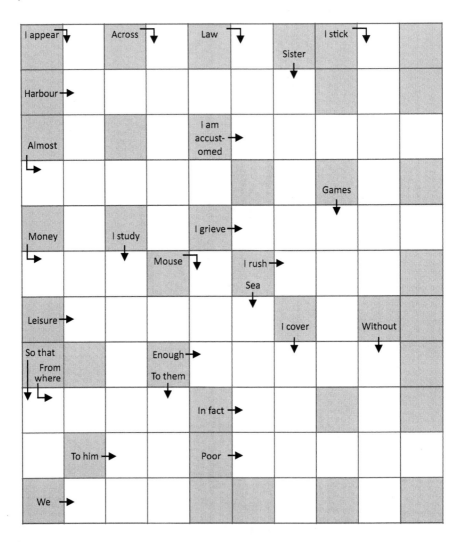

45   Building blocks

Solve the riddle by answering all the statements made below. As you answer each question, insert a letter in the grid underneath, where you will see two words formed. You may need to refer to Word List 3 for help.

Word 1

1.   My first is in lutum and also in labor.
2.   My second is in mare but not in sermo.
3.   My third is in pater but not in mater.
4.   My fourth is triple in triclinium.
5.   My fifth is in sino and also in foedus.

Word 2

1.   My first is in quo and double in quoque.
2.   My second is double in lupus and humus.
3.   My third is in ad and also in ante.
4.   My fourth is in undique but not in ubique.
5.   My fifth is in spero but not in spes.
6.   My sixth is arena's top and tail.
7.   My seventh is in postea and double in tot.
8.   My eighth is in fluo but not in fleo.
9.   My ninth is in saxum and also in sicut.

My whole is a building block.

1	2	3	4	5

1	2	3	4	5	6	7	8	9

46   Crossword

The clues are in English but the answers are all in Latin. If you need help, refer to Word List 3 at the back of the book.

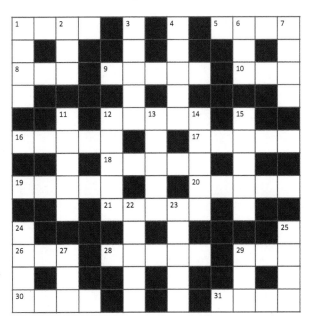

ACROSS

1.   Lacrima (4)
5.   Fluo (4)
8.   Lutum (3)
9.   Coepi (5)
10. Bellum (3)
12. Celeritas (5)
16. Viso (5)
17. Occurro (1,4)
18. Ara (5)
19. Lupus quidam (1,4)
20. Illuc (5)
21. Quadraginta (5)
26. Ita vero (3)
28. Postquam (5)
29. Taberna (3)
30. Canto (4)
31. Fabula (4)

DOWN

1.   Sepulcrum (4)
2.   Atque (3)
3.   Fleo (1,4)
4.   Candidus (5)
6.   Ius (3)
7.   Labor (4)
11. Consisto (1,4)
12. Baculum (5)
13. Ineo (5)
14. Sordidus (5)
15. Septem (5)
22. Offero (5)
23. Tracto (5)
24. Oculus and oculus (4)
25. Modo (4)
27. Filius (3)
29. Aeger (3)

*Note: where a verb is the clue, such as **iaceo - I lie**, the word **I** may be omitted or included in your answer.*

47 Workers

Among the Roman workers listed below, some have an easier life than others. They may be written across, down, or even diagonally. Oh yes, they could also be written backwards! See if you can find them all.

L	X	C	U	M	M	E	R	C	X	S	H	U	S	R	M
I	U	S	C	E	B	S	E	N	A	T	O	R	T	L	S
B	S	R	A	D	T	C	L	I	E	N	S	H	G	I	S
E	I	A	N	I	T	O	R	M	A	T	P	H	G	U	O
R	N	A	D	C	U	S	U	T	A	G	E	L	E	G	R
T	E	S	I	U	P	C	L	T	V	B	S	I	U	O	D
U	V	H	D	S	A	X	A	T	R	U	C	A	T	S	G
S	U	I	A	T	R	V	A	U	R	I	G	A	L	O	L
S	I	N	T	G	E	S	T	R	P	E	R	L	O	D	A
F	U	L	U	S	N	O	C	T	I	O	G	L	B	R	D
R	U	V	S	I	S	I	V	I	L	S	T	I	R	E	I
F	L	O	R	I	B	P	A	U	P	E	R	C	N	C	A
C	A	M	M	E	R	C	A	T	O	R	I	N	N	A	T
B	U	B	N	S	S	I	D	L	E	V	I	A	T	S	O
I	U	D	E	X	B	T	R	D	I	C	T	A	T	O	R
L	C	I	V	R	I	V	I	S	V	I	L	I	C	U	S

ANCILLA	DICTATOR	LEGATUS	REGINA
AURIGA	FABER	LIBERTUS	SACERDOS
CANDIDATUS	GLADIATOR	MEDICUS	SENATOR
CAUPO	HOSPES	MERCATOR	SERVUS
CIVIS	IANITOR	ORATOR	VILICUS
CLIENS	IUDEX	PARENS	
CONSUL	IUVENIS	PAUPER	

48   Crossword

The clues are in Latin but the answers are all in English. If you need help, you can use any of the word lists at the back.

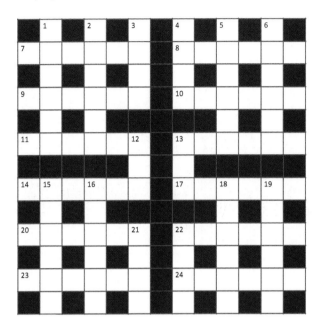

ACROSS

7. Appareo (6)
8. Foedus (6)
9. Laudo (6)
10. Sacerdos (6)
11. Attendo (6)
13. Malo (6)
14. Gemo (1,5)
17. Tractat (6)
20. Non unus (3,3)
22. Lente (6)
23. Et iaceo (3,3)
24. Consentio (1,5)

DOWN

1. Animus (6)
2. Cupio (6)
3. Verus (4)
4. Consisto (4)
5. Constituo (6)
6. Gusto (1,5)
12. Fragor (3)
13. Pono (3)
15. Humus (6)
16. Aut tantum (2,4)
18. Satis (6)
19. Orator (6)
21. Etiam (4)
22. Navis (4)

*Note: where a verb is the clue, such as **iaceo - I lie**, the word **I** may be omitted or included in your answer.*

49   Latin crossword

The clues are in English but the answers are all in Latin. If you need help, refer to Word List 3 at the back of the book.

ACROSS

1. Sleep (6)
4. I learn (5)
7. Come (3)
9. I grieve (5)
10. She (4)
12. But (3)
13. Human (4)
15. I buy (3)
16. Thus (3)
17. I love (3)
18. Goddess (3)
21. Her (3)
22. Once (4)
24. Cow (3)
28. Hope (4)
29. Name (5)
30. Soon (3)
31. Mud (5)
32. Shoulder (6)

DOWN

1. Home (5)
2. I prefer (4)
3. Wife (4)
4. About (2)
5. I am accustomed (5)
6. Speaker (6)
8. I rejoice (6)
11. Ten (5)
13. Today (5)
14. You are (2)
17. I walk (6)
19. But (2)
20. Consul (6)
23. He is (2,3)
25. Year (5)
26. For (4)
27. Love (4)
30. 2000 (2)

50   Cryptic Latin crossword

The answers to this terrible torture are all in Latin. If you need help, you can use any of the word lists at the back of the book.

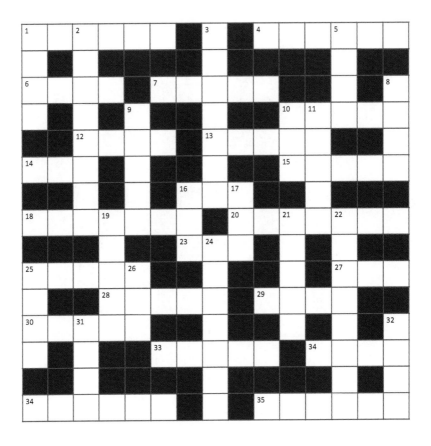

ACROSS

1. Rag for a racket? (6)
4. Spanner in the works for a mum without direction (6)
6. Concoct original around this little number (4)
7. Slave too upset to say hello (5)
10. I get in trouble as I come in (5)
12. What – a pound for that? (4)
13. A rush away from the East with this weapon (5)
14. Long time for you and the princess (3)
15. French friend goes to California for his girl (5)
16. Back to front? It makes no difference at the altar (3)
18. Fall dramatically in disarray at the holy place (7)
20. Car sticker brings joy (7)
23. Foreign gold for beggar (3)
25. Seems companion's on the way (5)
27. Ermine for a robber? (3)
28. Snub casts shadow in East (5)
29. Space in arena with no direction to go (4)
30. Consider one hundred for ten (5)
33. Australian gentleman's back to listen (5)
34. A pure-hearted lad (4)
35. Summer seat is ready for us (6)
36. Confused as I can at home (2,4)

DOWN

1. What if loser finds the bloom? (4)
2. Sounds like an ancient ham before its time (8)
3. Help cur to be beautiful (7)
5. Its previous state was on the way out (4)
8. Goes round to Royal Academy (4)
9. Annihilates just about nothing (5)
10. I give thanks in such a way (3)
11. In mad dash, for it is the only answer (3,2)
16. A doctor's in love (3)
17. I do this as I did a while back (3)
19. Almost there when dad takes directions (5)
21. Shady hesitation with underwear (5)
22. No saint to flaunt bias in play (2,6)
24. Thing was confusing for rat and prophet (3,4)
25. Fall into messed up musical ending (4)
26. Count me in (3)
31. Sarcastic start for tomorrow (4)
32. No harm at all in weapons (4)

51   Sudoku

You know how Sudoku works. All you have to do is to place numbers one to nine in each vertical and horizontal line and then make sure that each number appears once in each of the nine 3x3 squares. The difference here is that this is Roman Sudoku! In this challenge, you use the numbers as below.

Roman numbers

1	2	3	4	5	6	7	8	9
I	II	III	IV	V	VI	VII	VIII	IX

Good luck – prosit!

	IV	I	IX			VI	V	
	II				V	IX		
V	III			IV	II		I	VIII
	I			II			IX	
VIII		IV				I		V
	V			IX			VII	
	VI	II			IX		VIII	VII
	VIII				III		VI	
	VII	III		VIII		V	IV	

52   Say or stay

Below you will find two grids and a set of double clues. Your job is to put the right answers in the right boxes of the right grids. You may notice that all the letters of the shorter words go into the longer ones above or below them along with one more letter, which should make life quite easy for you. Good luck.

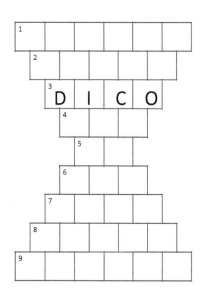

1.   I know it (4,2) *** I overcome (6)
2.   I hope (5) *** I learn (5)
3.   I-say (4) *** Late (4)
4.   Them (3) *** I hate (3)
5.   I give (2) *** I go (2)
6.   Two (3) *** I buy (3)
7.   Nobody (4) *** I play (4)
8.   I-stay (5) *** I praise (5)
9.   I close (6) *** And I do not love (3,3)

53   Matching animals

There are two parts to this puzzle, which features different sorts of animals in English and Latin. First off, you should try to match the animals on the left with the Latin words on the right in the lists below.

Bird	Asinus
Cat	Avis
Cow	Bos
Dog	Canis
Donkey	Elephantus
Elephant	Equus
Fish	Feles
Horse	Homo
Human	Leo
Lion	Lupus
Mouse	Mus
Sheep	Ovis
Sparrow	Passer
Wolf	Piscis

And now to the grid, where you should find the Latin animals all hidden away. Words may go across, backwards, up, down or diagonally.

V	U	N	F	E	D	L	O	S	I	V	A	V	I	R	O	T	E
U	H	Q	U	U	S	E	V	U	P	S	I	T	E	R	A	R	L
H	O	M	D	B	O	A	I	S	S	I	C	S	I	P	L	E	E
U	M	U	O	R	M	U	S	T	B	N	S	T	E	U	R	S	P
S	O	S	R	E	E	F	E	L	E	A	R	V	P	U	L	E	H
L	U	R	E	N	G	S	E	U	P	E	Q	U	U	N	O	N	A
E	O	N	E	L	E	O	N	L	E	N	S	T	L	P	A	N	N
T	T	G	I	T	I	G	R	I	E	V	U	L	P	U	N	R	T
E	R	P	P	S	I	T	T	A	C	S	U	U	Q	E	U	S	U
P	I	S	C	I	A	V	I	C	A	N	I	S	E	H	N	U	S

54   Wise advice

Put your answers to the clues in the table below. Some boxes are numbered and where you see these numbers appear elsewhere on this page, they always represent the same letters. Your final job is to reveal a very old Latin-English joke in the table at the bottom, which has amused countless of us in the past and may still make you groan aloud today.

1	1		5		**2**	3		4		13	**3**	6	13		1	
4	2	9	1		10	17			**5**	15	12		4		8	
6	3	3	9				**7**	18	16		13	**8**		5		3
9	3							10	11	**10**	14			10	11	17
11	18		8	**12**	13	1		8	**13**	1		6		15		
14	14	5					14	5	11	**15**		9			9	3
16	2	16	6				16		16		**17**	6		15		3
18	18	4			3		**19**	6			5	10	10			5
20	7	7			**21**	15			11	5	**22**	18			2	9
23	12	10	16		10				**24**	12	10	9			2	10

1. Boy (4)	13. Money (7)
2. Wood (5)	14. Repeatedly (9)
3. Innkeeper (5)	15. Ring (6)
4. I blame (8)	16 Dining room (10)
5. Unhappy (7)	17. Ash (5)
6. I can (6)	18. Wound (6)
7. Life (4)	19. Very quickly (9)
8. Family (4)	20. I drink (4)
9. Tomb (9)	21. Name (5)
10. I sleep (6)	22. Prayer (5)
11. Scarcely (3)	23. Bravely (8)
12. Top (4)	24. In vain (7)

3	5	11	1	5	10	■	9	7	16	■	3	9	7	■	9	7	16

55   Always a teacher

Look carefully at the grid below. The object of the puzzle is to find out which letter of the alphabet is represented by each of the 17 numbers used. You are given one word to start you off, so you can begin by entering any letters from this wherever they appear in the grid. Each word you make should be in good Latin. As you decode each letter, write it in the Letters deciphered table and cross it off in the Letters used table.

Letters deciphered

1	2	3	4	5	6	7	8	9	10	11	12	13	14	15	16	17
M	A	G	I	S	T	E	R									

Letters used

A	C	D	E	G	I	L	M	N	O	P	Q	R	S	T	U	V

56 Danger's above

Put your answers to the clues in the grids below. You may have one problem, however: there are two questions for each of the clues and you have to decide into which grid the right answers should go. Two words have been given to start you off. Bonam fortunam.

ACROSS

5. ~~Danger~~ (9) **** General (9)
6. Six (3) **** Pig (3)
8. Wall (5) **** Judge (5)
9. With (3) **** His (3)
10. Apt (5) **** Ash (5)
11. I become (3) **** We (3)
13. I understand (9) **** Bedroom (9)

DOWN

1. Hope (4) **** Day (4)
2. Top (4) **** Three (4)
3. Mud (5) **** Door (5)
4. Not where (3,3) **** I overcome (6)
7. Everywhere (6) **** I put out (6)
8. Mouse (3) **** Law (3)
9. ~~Above~~ (5) **** Citizen (5)
11. I do not want (4) **** I weep (4)
12. Smell (4) **** I take (4)

57   Crossword

The clues are in Latin but the answers are all in English. If you need help, you can use any of the word lists at the back.

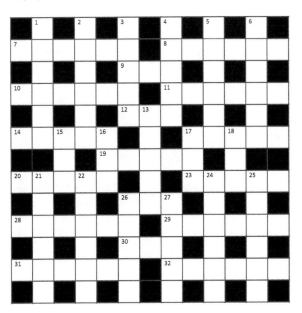

ACROSS

7. Schola (6)
8. Non aptus (3,3)
9. Iaceo (3)
10. Inquit ita (4,2)
11. Mater (6)
12. Cur (3)
14. Mors (5)
17. Litus (5)
19. Terra (5)
20. Alius (5)
23. Hostis (5)
26. Oculus (3)
28. Intro (1,5)
29. Paene (6)
30. Ars (3)
31. Dignitas (6)
32. Ita video (2,1,3)

DOWN

1. Cesso (1,5)
2. Nunc sedeo (3,3)
3. Sino (5)
4. Inimicus (5)
5. Sutura (6)
6. Appareo (6)
13. Festino (5)
15. Cinis (3)
16. Eam (3)
17. Illa (3)
18. Debeo (3)
21. Foedus (6)
22. Praedium (6)
24. Nomen est (4,2)
25. Dominus (6)
26. Erado (5)
27. Consumo ita (3,2)

*Note: where a verb is the clue, such as **iaceo - I lie**, the word **I** may be omitted or included in your answer.*

58   Latin crossword

The clues are in English but the answers are all in Latin. If you need help, refer to the word lists at the back of the book.

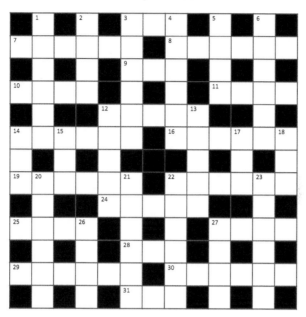

ACROSS

3. Pig (3)
7. Then when? (3,3)
8. I hate money (3,3)
9. Her (3)
10. Eight (4)
11. Without (4)
12. Dear (5)
14. Too much (6)
16. Always (6)
19. At once (6)
22. Tired (6)
24. Ear (5)
25. I wash (4)
27. Alas (4)
28. There (3)
29. But hurray (2,4)
30. Everywhere (6)
31. Thing (3)

DOWN

1. All together (6)
2. I lead (4)
3. If I was (2,4)
4. Sleep (6)
5. Day (4)
6. Then (6)
12. Senate house (5)
13. Home (5)
14. We (3)
15. My (3)
17. Foot (3)
18. Countryside (3)
20. I treat (6)
21. Woman (6)
22. Son (6)
23. Shoulder (6)
26. Task (4)
27. For (4)

59   Cryptic Latin crossword

The answers to this terrible torture are all in Latin. If you need help, you can use any of the word lists at the back of the book.

ACROSS

3. Chicken about this (3)
8. Moodier? There's no point sleeping! (6)
9. No, I am. That's all for now. (5,3)
10. Upset rite of passage (4)
11. Be silent to hold best card (5)
12. Sees it's about to be (4)
13. Useful limit for us is a mile away (6)
15. Bid zero for lookalike (6)
18. Not got no love for midday (3)
20. Drop business chief to move forward (7)
21. Watching pig I love is no silent matter (7)
23. So it should be in sickness and in health (3)
25. Student loses right to attend class (6)
28. Two questions due out but no date nor time also (6)
29. Could hear pulse well (4)
31. Pan is around the back (5)
32. Sense of lost bloom (4)
33. Game on for me now (4,4)
34. Lady's taken out two sugars again (6)
35. Rush to our return (3)

DOWN

1. Bravely heard in the dairy (8)
2. Love's back in Rome (4)
3. Short change in university garden (6)
4. Do no measurement so I collapse (7)
5. Call up foreign wine for army boss (6)
6. Farewell between the hills (4)
7. Bird is faster than the rest (6)
14. Bright enough, with zero clue (5)
16. If you go, go quickly (5)
17. Quietly beg for love (3)
18. Son's back for us (3)
19. And don't make that gulping noise (3)
20. Legend's pesky commencement (3)
22. Our lad takes us on countryside tribute (5,3)
24. Doorkeeper's disappeared into air (7)
26. Californian mule's in heaven (6)
27. USA set for high temperatures (6)
28. No time on the equator for asking (6)
30. Looks eccentric at the outset (4)
32. Carry saint out of wood (4)

60   Honeycomb

Look carefully at the grid below. Your job is to write your answers to the clues around the numbers, always beginning in the cell space immediately above the number. The difficulty for you is that some answers go clockwise around the number and some go anti-clockwise. Good luck in working out which is which.

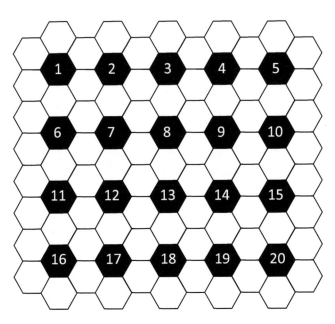

1.	Charioteer (6)	11.	Not law (3,3)
2.	Course (6)	12.	Wound (6)
3.	Tired (6)	13.	Sweet (6)
4.	Foot thing (3,3)	14.	Useful (6)
5.	And day (3,3)	15.	Says (6)
6.	He (is) one (2,4)	16.	Angry (6)
7.	Savage (6)	17.	None (6)
8.	But goddess (3,3)	18.	Kitchen (6)
9.	I lead back (6)	19.	Lance (6)
10.	I indicate (6)	20.	From where she (4,2)

Solutions

1 Mini crossword

```
I . . . I . S
S O L D I E R
A . . E . E .
Y . A S K . H
. N . I . . O
B E D R O O M
. W . E . . E
```

2 Latin mini

```
C U R . A G O
A . . . B . .
N O V U S . S
I . O . U . E
S . T A M E N
. . U . . . E
E A M . V O X
```

3 He's the boss

```
I R A
U B I
P E R
P E S
I B I
T U M
E G O
R E X
```

Iuppiter is the Latin name for Jupiter – the king of all the gods.

4 The lonely soldier

```
D O M I N U S
I . A . . . T
M I L E S . O
I . U . E . R
T . S E D E O
T . . . I . G
O S T E N D O
```

5 A happy task

```
L U D O . . .
A . I . I R A
E X E O . . N
T . S . I . I
U . . O L I M
S U M . L . U
. . . D E U S
```

6 Roman Emperors

```
A U G U S T U S . . . . . . . . C
N S E V E R U S A L E X A N D E R O
T . . . . N A J A R T I . . . . M
O . . . . . . . . . . O . . . M
N S . H A L U G I L A C . C . . O
I U V . A N A I T I M O D . L . D
N I E . D N . . N T . . E . . U
U L S U R E V E S S U I M I T P E S
S E P . I R . T . T . . I . . .
P R A . A O . A N . U . . A . . N
I U S N A N S Q A L S A K N . . A
U A I . T . U S U I R E B I T . I
S S A . I E . I . . L . . A . R
. U N N . G . D . . . E . V . . E
. C E . . . U . . . R . . . L
. R . A B L A G . . E . U . . A
A V I T E L L I U S N . . T A . V
M . C A R A C A L L A . . O H T O
```

7 Sudoku

III	II	IV	IX	VII	VIII	V	VI	I
V	VIII	VII	III	VI	I	II	IX	IV
I	VI	IX	II	V	IV	VIII	VII	III
II	IV	VI	VII	VIII	IX	III	I	V
VII	I	VIII	V	III	VI	IX	IV	II
IX	V	III	I	IV	II	VI	VIII	VII
IV	III	II	VI	IX	VII	I	V	VIII
VI	VII	V	VIII	I	III	IV	II	IX
VIII	IX	I	IV	II	V	VII	III	VI

8 Crossword

```
. A . B . S . D .
E N E R G E T I C
. D . A . E . N .
H . V . . . . C .
O N C E . W E A R
W . . . O . . Y .
. S . . A . U . N
M E S S E N G E R
. E . K . D . W .
```

9 Beware of the dog!

S	A	E	P	E			C	E	N	T	U	R	I	O
	B		O								R		A	
I		D	E	S	C	E	N	D	O		B		C	
N		T		A				E		S		E		
Q		A		E		A	B	E	O		D	O		
U		L		E				E		O				
I	L	L	A		U		E	O	S		E	M	O	
T		D	U	M		X				U				
		V					V	O	S					
	R	E	P	E	L	L	O		I					
F		N		X			C			Q				
A		I		E	U	M		I		E		U		
C	A	D	O		O		O		N	A	R	R	O	
I				N				U		A		D		
O		I	N	G	E	N	S		S		T			

The dog's name is Rufus.

10 Crossword

11 Cryptic Latin crossword

12 Arrowword

	E		D		E		I		E
I	S		I		X		R	E	X
		T	U	N	I	C	A		
S	U	A			T	U		I	D
T		N	A	M		P	O	N	O
A		D				I		G	
T	R	E	S		N	O	M	E	N
I		M	E		U			N	
M	I		C	U	M		E	S	T
		U			E	O		U	
C	L	A	M	O	R		S	U	M

13 A great man

P	E	R	I	C	U	L	U	M
		H	O	M	O			
P	E	C	U	N	I	A		
		A	S	C	E	N	D	O
	F	O	R	T	I	T	E	R
S	I	L	V	A				
	I	A	N	U	A			
	M	I	T	T	O			
	A	U	D	I	O			
F	E	M	I	N	A			
E	X	S	P	E	C	T	O	

Constantine the Great was the Roman emperor who introduced Christianity as a state religion.

14 It's your game

15 Latin crossword

	F		E		P		D	E	U	S
C	E	N	T	U	R	I	O			E
	R		M		O				U	
N	O	M	E	N		P	U	G	N	O
	C					B		U		
M	I	L	E	S		D	I	U	S	I
	T		S					S		
V	E	R	T	O		M	I	S	E	R
	R			C		P		C		
T		T	U	U	S	S	U	U	S	
E	H	E	U		R		A		M	

16 Crossword

17 Action speaks

B	D		I	N	V	E	N	I	O	Q	U	I	E	S	C	O	
O	I	G	U	F		T	A	C	E	O	V	U					O
	S	B	P		R			O	I	N	E	V	N	O	C		R
I	C		O	G	E	L			O		N	O			O	L	H	T
U	E		R	E	D	E	O	A	R		I		N		A	P	N
B	D	H	T		D	T		C	R		O	V		B	M	A	I
E	O	A	O	O	O	E		C	E	N	O		I		O	R	
O		B	O	E		N		I		C		T	P	E	T	O	C
	F	E	D	D		E	I	P	O		O	N	G	U	P		O
C	E	O	E	I		O	N	I	P	R	O	M	I	T	T	O	Q
U	S		C	R			C	O		C		V	E	R	T	O	U
R	T		O	C	O	N	I	C	I	O	T	C	E	P	S		O
O	I	M	R	O	D	P	T		O	N		O	R	O	B	A	L
	N		P		A	O		D	T	S	C	R	I	B	O	U
	O	A	S	C	E	N	D	O	A	E	X	C	I	T	O	O	B
O	M	E	G	A	U	D	E	O	R	N					C	M
	L	A	U	D	O	E	M	I	T	D		V	O	C	O	I	A
			O	E	V	A	C		O	E	N	A	M		D

18 Mini crossword

G	O	D	D	E	S	S
E	■	I	■	■	■	O
N	O	T	■	I	■	T
E	■	C	O	W	■	I
R	■	H	■	A	I	R
A	■	■	■	R	■	E
L	E	A	R	N	E	D

19 Latin mini

I	G	N	O	T	U	S
■	U	■	B	■	■	■
■	S	■	S	■	A	■
A	T	T	E	N	D	O
■	O	■	R	■	S	■
■	■	■	V	■	U	■
D	E	F	O	R	M	A

20 What do you mean?

```
I M P E D I O
    V I X
I N T E L L E G O
      I M P E R O
  S U P E R O
      L E N T E
R A P I O
    M A G I S T E R
      F R U S T R A
      S A L V E
L E C T U S
    D E I N D E
      A L I U S
```

The Latin expression *exempli gratia* means *for example* in English. It is normally just written as *eg*.

21 The abandoned flower

E	■	O	P	T	I	M	U	S
F	■	■	■	■	E	■	■	
F	L	O	S	■	■	U	■	E
U	■	C	R	A	S	■	■	X
G	■	I	■	M	■	■	■	T
I	■	N	O	L	O	■	■	R
O	■	U	■	R	O	T	A	
■	■	N	■	■	■	■	■	H
R	E	C	U	M	B	O	■	O

22 I recognise that!

S	T	R	E	N	U	E	■	A
I	■	■	■	R	■	G
M	■	V	■	V	A	L	E
U	■	D	E	C	E	M	■
L	■	N	■	R	■	V
■	A	D	H	U	C	■	I
S	E	R	O	■	S	■	N
E	■	E	■	■	■	C
X	A	G	N	O	S	C	O

23 Roman Gods

S	M	D	I	A	N	A				C	S		S
E	I		F	V	A	P	O	L	L	O	U	I	R
L	N		A	U			J	U	N	O	P	P	E
U	E	N	U	L		P	L	U	T	O		I	A	T
C	R	E	N	C	A	S	U	D	E	M	D	R	I
R	V	P	U	A	M	I	T	H	R	A	S	E	P	P
E	A	T	S	N					R		S	R	U
H	Y	U				A			S	C		O	J
	R	N		N	R	U	T	A	S			S	B
U	E			I	S	I	S			E	E	A
C				S	E	R	E	C		L	R	C
R		V	E	N	U	S			V		E	P	C
E						J	A	N	U	S	B	I	H
M		F	O	R	T	U	N	A			Y	N	U
A	E	S	C	U	L	A	P	I	U	S		C	A	S

24 Sudoku

VII	IV	I	IX	III	VIII	VI	V	II
VI	II	VIII	I	VII	V	IX	III	IV
V	III	IX	VI	IV	II	VII	I	VIII
III	I	VII	V	II	IV	VIII	IX	VI
VIII	IX	IV	III	VI	VII	I	II	V
II	V	VI	VIII	IX	I	IV	VII	III
I	VI	II	IV	V	IX	III	VIII	VII
IV	VIII	V	VII	I	III	II	VI	IX
IX	VII	III	II	VIII	VI	V	IV	I

25 Latin crossword

26 Members of a club

The three are Caesar, Crassus and Pompeius, who were all members of the First Triumvirate.

27 Crossword

28 Cryptic Latin crossword

29 Arrowword

30 Writer's block

Cornelius Tacitus was a famous historian who wrote about the emperors of Rome and the politics of the day.

31 There's a way

```
■ M E ■ E ■ C
N E M O ■ A U R A
■ U ■ ■ A ■ ■ A
■ S T U L T U S
■ ■ A ■ T ■ B
■ I M P E D I O
■ T ■ ■ R ■ ■ C
C E R A ■ D A T E
■ R ■ T ■ E ■ O
```

32 Latin crossword

```
F R A T E R ■ E C C E
E ■ ■ A ■ C ■ O ■
L A V O ■ S O M N U S
I ■ E ■ T ■ L ■ U
X ■ H I E M O ■ I ■ B
■ ■ I ■ M ■ N ■ L
I ■ C ■ P A U C I ■ F
A ■ U ■ L ■ S ■ U ■ E
M U L T U S ■ A M O R
■ U ■ M ■ D ■ ■ O
A R M A ■ M E N D A X
```

33 Crossword

```
■ ■ W ■ ■ ■ F
I D R A G ■ F I F T Y
■ O ■ T ■ E ■ V ■ E
A N D C A N ■ E A R
■ O ■ H ■ D ■ H ■ R
■ T ■ O ■ L ■ U ■ I
■ K ■ U ■ E ■ N ■ F
■ N O T ■ S A D A I R
■ O ■ F ■ S ■ R ■ E
T W O O R ■ R E A D Y
■ ■ R ■ ■ ■ D
```

34 What are you like?

```
I N O B I L I S U T O T O P B U
G D I F F I C I L I S   C R O T
N P R A   C A R U S   I C I N I
A L A C   S U U T R O M U M U L
V E T I S S U S S E F M P U S I
U N U L U U   S   E O A S U S
S U S I T G   S U   R B T S D U
U S U S O N S U T   O I U U I C
M I T U N O I N A   X L S T G I
R N N T G L L I R     I   I I T
I F E L I X A V A R U S   C R S
F E T U A   T I P S U U T A F U
N L N T   T   D   A   T   R
I I O S   M U L T U S C
  X C       S S U T S E L O M
I N V I T U S U M I T P O R
```

35 Mini crossword

```
■ R ■ A ■ O ■
I E S C A P E
■ C ■ T ■ I ■
S O N ■ I N N
■ V ■ W ■ I ■
S E N A T O R
■ R ■ R ■ N ■
```

36 Mini Latin crossword

```
■ A ■ H ■ I ■
U N D I Q U E
■ C ■ C ■ V ■
V I R ■ V E R
■ L ■ E ■ N ■
O L F A C I O
■ A ■ S ■ S ■
```

37 All at home

```
            M A T E R
      H O S P E S
            D O M I N A
      I A N I T O R
            F I L I U S
  I U V E N I S
          A N C I L L A
      M A R I T U S
  S E R V U S
          M A T E R
```

Aedificium means a building. They all live in one house.

38 What?

```
I N V O C O ■ S I N O
G ■ I ■ A ■ V ■ N ■ R
I S T E P U E R ■ D
T ■ U ■ U ■ H ■ A ■ O
U P T O N
R E ■ ■ X C
■ R Q P I U
G O U A E R
E ■ L I B E R T U S
N ■ S D N A U
S P E S ■ D E N S U S
```

39 A challenge in the arena

40 Latin crossword

41 A top place

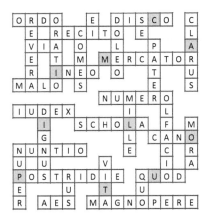

Capitolium was the name of the Capitoline Hill in Rome, where the great temple of Jupiter was situated.

42 Crossword

43 Cryptic Latin crossword

44 Arrowword

```
  A   T   I     H
P O R T U S   A
P   A   S O L E O
P A E N E   R   R
R   S   D O L E O
A E S   M   R U O
O T I U M   D
  U   S A T I S
U N D E   R E   I
T   E I   E G E N S
  N O S     O   E
```

45 Building blocks

```
L A P I S    Q U A D R A T U S
```

Lapis quadratus means squared stone, referring to the dressed stone with which the Romans built their buildings.

46 Crossword

```
T E A R . I . W . F L O W
O . N . . W . H . A . O
M U D . B E G I N . W A R
B . . . E . T . . . . . K
. . I . S P E E D . S . .
V I S I T . N . I M E E T
. . T . A L T A R . V . .
A W O L F . E . T H E R E
. P . F O R T Y . N . . .
E . . . F . R . . . . . O
Y E S . A F T E R . I N N
E . O . E . A . . L . L
S I N G . R . T . P L A Y
```

47 Workers

```
L . . M . . . . . H . . .
I . C E . S E N A T O R .
B S . A D . C L I E N S .
E I A N I T O R . . P . .
R N . D C . S U T A G E L . R
T E . I U P C . . . S . O
U V . D S A . A . . T S G
S U . A . R . A U R I G A . O L
S I . T E . . P E R L . D A
. U L U S N O C . O G L . R D
. V S S . . . . I . E I
F . R . P A U P E R C N C A
. A M E R C A T O R I N . A T
. B . S . . . . V . A S O
I U D E X . . D I C T A T O R
. . R . . S V I L I C U S
```

48 Crossword

```
. S . D . T . S . D . I
A P P E A R . T R E A T Y
. I . S . U . O . C . A
P R A I S E . P R I E S T
. I . R . . . . . D . T
A T T E N D . P R E F E R
. . . . . I . U . . . .
I G R O A N . T R E A T S
. R . R . . . . N . A
N O T O N E . S L O W L Y
. U . N . V . H . U . K
A N D L I E . I A G R E E
. D . Y . N . P . H . R
```

49 Latin crossword

```
S O M N U S . . D I S C O
E . A . X . A G E . O . R
D O L E O . . A . I L L A
E . O . R . U . . E . T
S . D . S E D . H O M O
. E . E . . E M O . . . R
. S I C . A M O . D E A
C . . E A M . . . I . T
O L I M . B O S . E . . A
N . S . U . . E . A . N
S P E S . L . N O M E N
U . S . M O X . I . O . U
L U T U M . . U M E R U S
```

50 Cryptic Latin crossword

```
F R A G O R . P . P A R E N S
L . N . . . U . . . . X .
O C T O . S A L V E . I . R
S . E . N . C . . I N T R O
. Q U I D . H A S T A . T
D I U . H . E . A M I C A
. A . I . A R A . I .
T E M P L U M . G A U D I U M
. . A . O R O . M . N .
C O M E S . E . B . F U R
A . . N U B E S . A R E A
D E C E M . E . A . B . A
O . R . A U R I S . P U E R
. A . . . . A . . L . M
A E S T U S . T . I N C A S A
```

51 Sudoku

VII	IV	I	IX	III	VIII	VI	V	II
VI	II	VIII	I	VII	V	IX	III	IV
V	III	IX	VI	IV	II	VII	I	VIII
III	I	VII	V	II	IV	VIII	IX	VI
VIII	IX	IV	III	VI	VII	I	II	V
II	V	VI	VIII	IX	I	IV	VII	III
I	VI	II	IV	V	IX	III	VIII	VII
IV	VIII	V	VII	I	III	II	VI	IX
IX	VII	III	II	VIII	VI	V	IV	I

52 Say or stay

SCIO ID
DISCO
DICO
ODI
DO
DUO
LUDO
LAUDO
CLAUDO

SUPERO
SPERO
SERO
EOS
EO
EMO
NEMO
MANEO
NEC AMO

53 Matching animals

Bird	Avis
Cat	Feles
Cow	Bos
Dog	Canis
Donkey	Asinus
Elephant	Elephantus
Fish	Piscis
Horse	Equus
Human	Homo
Lion	Leo
Mouse	Mus
Sheep	Ovis
Sparrow	Passer
Wolf	Lupus

```
. . . . . O S I V A . R . E
. H . . . . V . . . E . . L
O . B . . I . S I C S I P L E
M O M U S . . . S . . U . P
S O S . . F . . A . . P . H
U . . . E P . U . . . A
. N L E O . L . S . . . N
. I . . . E . . . . T
. S . . . . S U U Q E . U
. A . C A N I S . . S
```

54 Wise advice

```
P U E R ■ S I L V A ■ C A U P O
V I T U P E R O ■ I N F E L I X
P O S S U M ■ V I T A ■ G E N S
S E P U L C R U M ■ D O R M I O
V I X ■ A P E X ■ P E C U N I A
I D E N T I D E M ■ A N U L U S
T R I C L I N I U M ■ C I N I S
V U L N U S ■ C E L E R R I M E
B I B O ■ N O M E N ■ V O T U M
F O R T I T E R ■ F R U S T R A
```

```
S E M P E R ■ U B I ■ S U B ■ U B I
```

Always wear underwear.

55 Always a teacher

```
■ Q ■ A ■ I ■ D I E S
C U R M I T T O ■ ■ I
■ A ■ O ■ A ■ ■ I N
A D O R O ■ E V A D O
■ R ■ ■ R ■ I ■ E
L A U D O ■ A R E N A
■ T ■ I ■ G ■ ■ T
M U R U S ■ E I C I O
O ■ S ■ ■ A ■ P ■ D
N ■ ■ M A G I S T E R
S I N E ■ O ■ A ■ M
```

56 Danger's above

```
S ■ T ■ ■ L ■ S ■
P E R I C U L U M
E ■ E ■ ■ T ■ P ■
S U S ■ I U D E X
■ B ■ C U M ■ R ■
C I N I S ■ N O S
■ Q ■ V ■ ■ O ■ U
C U B I C U L U M
■ E ■ S ■ ■ O ■ O
```

```
D ■ A ■ ■ I ■ N ■
I M P E R A T O R
E ■ E ■ ■ N ■ N ■
S E X ■ M U R U S
■ X ■ S U A ■ B ■
A P T U S ■ F I O
■ O ■ P ■ ■ L ■ D
I N T E L L E G O
■ O ■ R ■ ■ O ■ R
```

57 Crossword

	I		N		A		E		S		A	
S	C	H	O	O	L		N	O	T	A	P	T
	E		W		L	I	E		I		P	
S	A	Y	S	S	O		M	O	T	H	E	R
	S		I		W	H	Y		C		A	
D	E	A	T	H		U		S	H	O	R	E
		S		E	A	R	T	H		W		
O	T	H	E	R		R		E	N	E	M	Y
	R		S		E	Y	E		A		A	
I	E	N	T	E	R		A	L	M	O	S	T
	A		A		A	R	T		E		T	
S	T	A	T	U	S		S	O	I	S	E	E
	Y		E		E		O		S		R	

58 Latin crossword

	C		D		S	U	S		D		D	
T	U	M	U	B	I		O	D	I	A	E	S
	N		C		E	A	M		E		I	
O	C	T	O		R		N		S	I	N	E
	T			C	A	R	U	S			D	
N	I	M	I	U	M		S	E	M	P	E	R
O		E		R				D	E		U	
S	T	A	T	I	M		F	E	S	S	U	S
	R			A	U	R	I	S			M	
L	A	V	O		L		L		E	H	E	U
	C		N		I	B	I		N		R	
A	T	E	U	G	E		U	B	I	Q	U	E
	O		S		R	E	S		M		S	

59 Cryptic Latin crossword

	F		A		H	I	C		I		V		P	
D	O	R	M	I	O		O	M	N	I	A		I	A	M
	R		O		R		N		V		L		S	
I	T	E	R		T	A	C	E	O		E	S	S	E
	I				U		I		C				E	
U	T	I	L	I	S		D		O	F	F	E	R	O
	E		U			N	O	N		U			R	
P	R	O	C	E	D	O		E	V	I	G	I	L	O
E		E			S	I	C		I				A	
S	C	H	O	L	A		A		Q	U	O	Q	U	E
	A			E		N		U					D	
B	E	N	E		S	P	I	N	A		F	L	O	S
L		C		T		T		E		E		R		
N	U	N	C	L	U	D	O		R	U	R	S	U	S
	M		E		S		R	U	O		O		S	

60 Honeycomb

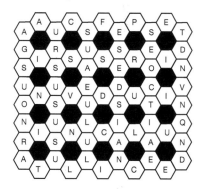

Word Lists Latin to English

Word List 1

ab	from	duco	I lead
abeo	I go away	dum	while
absum	I am absent	eam	her
accipio	I receive	ego	I
ad	towards	eheu	alas
advenio	I arrive	emo	I buy
ago	I do	eo	there
ambulo	I walk	eos	them
amo	I love	equus	horse
animus	spirit	erat	was
ascendo	I climb	erro	I wander
atrium	hall	es	you are
audio	I hear	esse	to be
bene	well	est	is
bibo	I drink	et	and
cado	I fall	eum	him
caelum	sky	ex	out of
canis	dog	excito	I arouse
capio	I take	exeo	I leave
caveo	I beware	exit	leaves
ceno	I dine	exspecto	I wait for
centurio	centurion	facio	I do
cinis	ash	femina	woman
clamo	I shout	ferociter	fiercely
clamor	shouting	festino	I hurry
conicio	I hurl	filia	daughter
conspicio	I see	fortis	brave
consumo	I eat	fortiter	bravely
contendo	I march	fragor	din
convenio	I meet	fugio	I flee
convoco	I call together	gaudeo	I rejoice
coquo	I cook	gemo	I groan
cubiculum	bedroom	gero	I wear
cum	with	habeo	I have
cupio	I desire	habito	I live
cur	why	hic	this
curo	I look after	hodie	today
curro	I run	homo	human
debeo	I owe	iaceo	I lie
descendo	I go down	ianua	door
deus	god	ibi	there
dico	I say	id	it
dies	day	illa	she
dimitto	I dismiss	ille	he
discedo	I leave	in	in
diu	(for a) long time	incito	I rouse up
do	I give	ingens	huge
dominus	master	inquit	says
domus	home	intro	I enter
dormio	I sleep	invenio	I find

ipsa	herself	rex	king
ira	anger	rideo	I smile
is	he	rogo	I ask
iubeo	I order	saepe	often
iuvo	I help	saluto	I greet
laboro	I work	scribo	I write
lacrimo	I cry	se	himself
laetus	happy	secum	with them
laudo	I praise	sed	but
lego	I read	sedeo	I sit
ludo	I play	senex	old man
ludus	game	servo	I serve
malus	bad	si	if
maneo	I stay	silva	wood
me	me	specto	I look at
mi	my	statim	at once
miles	soldier	sto	I stand
miser	sad	strenuus	energetic
mitto	I send	sua	his/her
mons	mountain	subito	suddenly
mox	soon	sum	I am
nam	for	sunt	are
narro	I tell	surgo	I rise up
nomen	name	suus	his/her
novus	new	taceo	I am silent
nox	night	tamen	however
nullus	none	tandem	at last
num	surely not	te	you (singular)
nuntius	messenger	teneo	I hold
olim	once	timeo	I fear
omnia	everything	toga	toga
omnis	all	trado	I hand over
ostendo	I show	tres	three
panis	bread	tu	you (singular)
paro	I prepare	tum	then
pecunia	money	tunica	tunic
per	through	tuus	your
periculum	danger	ubi	where
pes	foot	unus	one
peto	I seek	urbs	city
poeta	poet	venio	I come
pono	I put	verbero	I beat
porto	I carry	verto	I turn
pro	in front of	via	road
procedo	I proceed	vicinus	neighbouring
promitto	I send forward	video	I see
puer	boy	villa	house
pugno	I fight	voco	I call
quaero	I ask	volo	I want
quam	how	vos	you (plural)
quiesco	I rest	votum	prayer
quod	because	vox	voice
reddo	I give back	vulnus	wound
redeo	I go back		
repello	I push back	(208 words)	

Word List 2

accedo	I approach	ea	she
adhuc	up to now	ecce	look
adiuvo	I help	effugio	I escape
adsum	I am present	eo	I go
aeternus	endless	eram	I was
age	come	et	also
ager	field	etiam	even
agnosco	I recognise	euge	hurray
agricola	farmer	evigilo	I watch out for
aliquid	something	excipio	I take out
alius	other	exerceo	I exercise
alter	another	extraho	I drag out
amor	love	facilis	easy
anulus	ring	fama	fame
aperio	I open	fatuus	foolish
apex	top	felix	happy
appropinquo	I approach	fero	I bear
area	area	ferox	fierce
arma	armour	fessus	tired
ars	art	flos	flower
at	but	forma	form
attendo	I attend	fossa	ditch
aura	air	frater	brother
auris	ear	frigidus	cold
aut	or	frustra	in vain
avarus	greedy	gusto	I taste
bonus	good	hasta	spear
bos	cow	hiemo	I spend winter
calidus	hot	hortus	garden
carus	dear	hostis	enemy
casa	house	iam	already
castra	camp	id est	it is
cera	wax	ignavus	cowardly
cesso	I cease	ignotus	unknown
circumspecto	I look around	immobilis	not moving
colonus	farmer	impedio	I prevent
commotus	upset	imperator	general
consilium	advice	impero	I order
contentus	content	infelix	unhappy
coquus	cook	infirmus	unwell
cras	tomorrow	intellego	I understand
cuncti	all together	inter	between
da	give (singular)	invitus	unwilling
date	give (plural)	iratus	angry
de	about	ita	so
dea	goddess	iter	journey
decem	ten	iterum	again
deinde	then	latus	wide
depono	I put down	lavo	I wash
difficilis	difficult	lectus	couch
divinus	divine	lente	slowly
doctus	learned	leo	lion
duo	two	litus	shore

longus	long	quattuor	four
luceo	I shine	qui	who
lux	light	quingenti	five hundred
magister	master	quinquaginta	fifty
melior	better	quinque	five
mendax	liar	quis	who
mensa	table	rapio	I snatch
meus	my	recumbo	I recline
molestus	annoying	res	thing
moneo	I warn	rosa	rose
mors	death	rota	wheel
mortuus	dead	rusticus	from the country
multus	much	sacer	holy
nauta	sailor	salve	hello
navis	ship	scio	I know
nec	and not	sero	late
neco	I kill	sex	six
nemo	nobody	signum	sign
neque	and not	simul	at once
nescio	I do not know	somnus	sleep
nobilis	noble	strenue	energetically
nolo	I do not want	stultus	stupid
non	not	sub	under
nubes	cloud	summus	the top of
nunc	now	supero	I overcome
ob	on account of	tacitus	silent
observo	I observe	tale	such
occupatus	busy	talis	such
octo	eight	tam	so
odi	I hate	tantum	only
onus	task	templum	temple
optimus	best	tempto	I try
oro	I beg	terra	earth
os	mouth	territus	terrified
paratus	ready	totus	whole
pars	part	traho	I drag
parvus	small	tristis	sad
pauci	few	turba	crowd
pax	peace	ubi	when
plaudo	I applaud	umbra	shadow
plaustrum	wagon	unda	wave
plenus	full	utilis	useful
porta	door	vale	goodbye
possum	I can	vehiculum	vehicle
post	after	vendo	I sell
praeterea	besides	verbum	word
primum	at first	verus	true
primus	first	vinco	I conquer
princeps	leader	vinum	wine
pugna	fight	vix	scarcely
pulvis	dust		
purgo	I cleanse	(208 words)	

Word List 3

ad	to	egens	poor
adeo	I go towards	ei	to him
aedificium	building	eicio	I eject
aeger	ill	eis	to them
aes	money	evado	I escape
aestus	heat	faber	craftsman
ancilla	slave girl	fabula	play
annus	year	filius	son
ante	before	fio	I become
anxietas	anxiety	fleo	I weep
appareo	I appear	fluo	I flow
aptus	apt	foedus	treaty
ara	altar	fur	thief
arena	arena	gens	family
atque	and	gladiator	gladiator
aula	palace	haereo	I stick
auriga	charioteer	hic	here
baculum	staff	hospes	guest
bellum	war	humilis	lowly
candidatus	candidate	humus	ground
candidus	white	ianitor	doorkeeper
cano	I sing	identidem	repeatedly
canto	I sing	igitur	therefore
caput	head	illuc	there
caupo	innkeeper	in	into, in
celeritas	speed	ineo	I enter
celerrime	very quickly	inimicus	enemy
circum	around	insula	island
civis	citizen	invoco	I call on
clarus	clear	iste	that
claudo	I close	ita	thus
cliens	client	ita vero	yes
coepi	I begin	iudex	judge
comes	comrade	ius	law
consisto	I stop	iuvenis	young man
constituo	I decide	labor	work
consul	consul	lacrima	tear
cotidie	daily	lapis	stone
curia	senate house	legatus	ambassador
cursus	course	libertus	freedman
custos	guard	ludi	games
decido	I fall down	lupus	wolf
densus	thick	lutum	mud
dictator	dictator	magnus	great
dignus	worthy	magnopere	greatly
disco	I learn	malo	I prefer
doleo	I grieve	mare	sea
domina	mistress	maritus	husband
donum	gift	mater	mother
dulcis	sweet	medicus	doctor
eas	them	mercator	merchant

mille	thousand	rus	countryside
modo	only	sacerdos	priest
mora	delay	satis	enough
mulier	woman	saxum	rock
murus	wall	schola	school
mus	mouse	se	themselves
nimium	too much	sedes	home
nos	we	senator	senator
numero	I count	sententia	opinion
nuntio	I announce	septem	seven
nuper	recently	sepulcrum	tomb
occupo	I seize	sermo	conversation
occurro	I meet	servus	slave
oculus	eye	sicut	just as
offero	I offer	sine	without
olfacio	I smell	sino	I allow
oratio	speech	soleo	I am accustomed
orator	speaker	sordidus	dirty
ordo	series	soror	sister
otium	leisure	spero	I hope
paene	almost	spes	hope
parens	parent	sterto	I snore
pater	father	studeo	I study
patria	fatherland	tabella	table
pauper	poor man	taberna	inn
placide	calmly	tego	I cover
poculum	cup	tollo	I raise
portus	harbour	tot	so many
postea	afterwards	tracto	I treat
postquam	after	trans	across
postridie	the next day	triclinium	dining room
puer	slave	ubique	everywhere
quadraginta	forty	umerus	shoulder
quadratus	squared	unde	from where
quid	what	undique	from everywhere
quidam	a	ut	so that
quo	to where	veho	I carry
quod	which	ver	spring
quomodo	how	veto	I forbid
quoque	also	via	way
re	in fact	vilicus	steward
re vera	truly	vir	man
recito	I recite	viso	I visit
recupero	I recover	vita	life
recuso	I refuse	vitupero	I blame
regina	queen		
removeo	I remove	(195 words)	
ruo	I rush		

Word List 4

adoro	I adore	orator	talker
amica	girlfriend	ovis	sheep
antequam	before	passer	sparrow
asinus	donkey	piscis	fish
avis	bird	praedium	estate
concido	I collapse	pulcher	beautiful
consentio	I agree	reduco	I lead back
culina	kitchen	rursus	again
dignitas	status	saevus	savage
elephantus	elephant	semper	always
enim	for	sic	thus
erado	erase	spina	spine
expono	I put out	sumo	I take
feles	cat	super	above
gaudium	joy	sus	pig
indico	I indicate	sutura	stitch
lancea	lance	tractat	treats
mea	my	uxor	wife
nihil	nothing		
odor	smell	(38 words)	

Word Lists English to Latin

Word List 1

I am	sum	I fall	cado
I am absent	absum	I fear	timeo
alas	eheu	fiercely	ferociter
all	omnis	I fight	pugno
and	et	I find	invenio
anger	ira	I flee	fugio
are	sunt	foot	pes
you are	es	for	nam
I arouse	excito	for a long time	diu
I arrive	advenio	from	ab
ash	cinis	game	ludus
I ask	quaero	I give	do
I ask	rogo	I give back	reddo
at last	tandem	I go away	abeo
at once	statim	I go back	redeo
bad	malus	I go down	descendo
to be	esse	god	deus
I beat	verbero	I greet	saluto
because	quod	I groan	gemo
bedroom	cubiculum	hall	atrium
I beware	caveo	I hand over	trado
boy	puer	happy	laetus
brave	fortis	I have	habeo
bravely	fortiter	he	ille
bread	panis	he	is
but	sed	I hear	audio
I buy	emo	I help	iuvo
I call	voco	her	eam
I call together	convoco	herself	ipsa
I carry	porto	him	eum
centurion	centurio	himself	se
city	urbs	his/her	sua
I climb	ascendo	his/her	suus
I come	venio	home	domus
I cook	coquo	I hold	teneo
I cry	lacrimo	horse	equus
danger	periculum	house	villa
daughter	filia	how	quam
day	dies	however	tamen
I desire	cupio	huge	ingens
din	fragor	human	homo
I dine	ceno	I hurl	conicio
I dismiss	dimitto	I hurry	festino
I do	ago	I	ego
I do	facio	if	si
dog	canis	in	in
door	ianua	in front of	pro
I drink	bibo	is	est
I eat	consumo	it	id
energetic	strenuus	king	rex
I enter	intro	at last	tandem
everything	omnia	I lead	duco

I leave	discedo	she	illa
I leave	exeo	I shout	clamo
leaves	exit	shouting	clamor
I lie	iaceo	I show	ostendo
I live	habito	I am silent	taceo
for a long time	diu	I sit	sedeo
I look after	curo	sky	caelum
I look at	specto	I sleep	dormio
I love	amo	I smile	rideo
I march	contendo	soldier	miles
master	dominus	soon	mox
me	me	spirit	animus
I meet	convenio	I stand	sto
messenger	nuntius	I stay	maneo
money	pecunia	suddenly	subito
mountain	mons	surely not	num
my	mi	I take	capio
name	nomen	I tell	narro
neighbouring	vicinus	them	eos
new	novus	with them	secum
night	nox	then	tum
none	nullus	there	eo
surely not	num	there	ibi
often	saepe	this	hic
old man	senex	three	tres
once	olim	through	per
at once	statim	for a long time	diu
one	unus	to be	esse
I order	iubeo	today	hodie
out of	ex	toga	toga
I owe	debeo	towards	ad
I play	ludo	tunic	tunica
poet	poeta	I turn	verto
I praise	laudo	voice	vox
prayer	votum	I wait for	exspecto
I prepare	paro	I walk	ambulo
I proceed	procedo	I wander	erro
I push back	repello	I want	volo
I put	pono	was	erat
I read	lego	I wear	gero
I receive	accipio	well	bene
I rejoice	gaudeo	where	ubi
I rest	quiesco	while	dum
I rise up	surgo	why	cur
road	via	with	cum
I rouse up	incito	with them	secum
I run	curro	woman	femina
sad	miser	wood	silva
I say	dico	I work	laboro
says	inquit	wound	vulnus
I see	conspicio	I write	scribo
I see	video	you (plural)	vos
I seek	peto	you (singular)	tu *or* te
I send	mitto	you are	es
I send forward	promitto	your	tuus
I serve	servo		
		(208 Latin words)	

Word List 2

about	de	door	porta
on account of	ob	I put down	depono
advice	consilium	I drag	traho
after	post	I drag out	extraho
again	iterum	dust	pulvis
air	aura	ear	auris
all together	cuncti	earth	terra
already	iam	easy	facilis
also	et	eight	octo
I am present	adsum	endless	aeternus
and not	nec	enemy	hostis
and not	neque	energetically	strenue
angry	iratus	I escape	effugio
annoying	molestus	even	etiam
another	alter	I exercise	exerceo
I applaud	plaudo	fame	fama
I approach	accedo	farmer	agricola
I approach	appropinquo	farmer	colonus
area	area	few	pauci
armour	arma	field	ager
art	ars	fierce	ferox
at first	primum	fifty	quinquaginta
at once	simul	fight	pugna
I attend	attendo	first	primus
I bear	fero	at first	primum
I beg	oro	five	quinque
besides	praeterea	five hundred	quingenti
best	optimus	flower	flos
better	melior	foolish	fatuus
between	inter	form	forma
brother	frater	four	quattuor
busy	occupatus	from the country	rusticus
but	at	full	plenus
camp	castra	garden	hortus
I can	possum	general	imperator
I cease	cesso	give (plural)	date
I cleanse	purgo	give (singular)	da
cloud	nubes	I go	eo
cold	frigidus	goddess	dea
come	age	good	bonus
I conquer	vinco	goodbye	vale
content	contentus	greedy	avarus
cook	coquus	happy	felix
couch	lectus	I hate	odi
from the country	rusticus	hello	salve
cow	bos	I help	adiuvo
cowardly	ignavus	holy	sacer
crowd	turba	hot	calidus
dead	mortuus	house	casa
dear	carus	five hundred	quingenti
death	mors	hurray	euge
difficult	difficilis	in vain	frustra
ditch	fossa	it is	id est
divine	divinus	journey	iter
I do not know	nescio	I kill	neco
I do not want	nolo	I know	scio

I do not know	nescio	small	parvus
late	sero	I snatch	rapio
leader	princeps	so	ita
learned	doctus	so	tam
liar	mendax	something	aliquid
light	lux	spear	hasta
lion	leo	I spend winter	hiemo
long	longus	stupid	stultus
look	ecce	such	tale
I look around	circumspecto	such	talis
love	amor	table	mensa
master	magister	I take out	excipio
mouth	os	task	onus
much	multus	I taste	gusto
my	meus	temple	templum
noble	nobilis	ten	decem
nobody	nemo	terrified	territus
not	non	then	deinde
and not	nec	thing	res
and not	neque	tired	fessus
not moving	immobilis	all together	cuncti
I do not know	nescio	tomorrow	cras
I do not want	nolo	top	apex
now	nunc	the top of	summus
I observe	observo	true	verus
on account of	ob	I try	tempto
at once	simul	two	duo
only	tantum	under	sub
I open	aperio	I understand	intellego
or	aut	unhappy	infelix
I order	impero	unknown	ignotus
other	alius	unwell	infirmus
I overcome	supero	unwilling	invitus
part	pars	up to now	adhuc
peace	pax	upset	commotus
I am present	adsum	useful	utilis
I prevent	impedio	vehicle	vehiculum
I put down	depono	wagon	plaustrum
ready	paratus	I do not want	nolo
I recline	recumbo	I warn	moneo
I recognise	agnosco	I was	eram
ring	anulus	I wash	lavo
rose	rosa	I watch out for	evigilo
sad	tristis	wave	unda
sailor	nauta	wax	cera
scarcely	vix	wheel	rota
I sell	vendo	when	ubi
shadow	umbra	who	qui
she	ea	who	quis
I shine	luceo	whole	totus
ship	navis	wide	latus
shore	litus	wine	vinum
sign	signum	I spend winter	hiemo
silent	tacitus	word	verbum
six	sex		
sleep	somnus	(208 Latin words)	
slowly	lente		

Word List 3

a	quidam	enough	satis
across	trans	I enter	ineo
I am accustomed	soleo	I escape	evado
after	postquam	everywhere	ubique
afterwards	postea	from everywhere	undique
I allow	sino	eye	oculus
almost	paene	I fall down	decido
also	quoque	family	gens
altar	ara	father	pater
ambassador	legatus	fatherland	patria
and	atque	I flow	fluo
I announce	nuntio	I forbid	veto
anxiety	anxietas	forty	quadraginta
I appear	appareo	freedman	libertus
apt	aptus	from everywhere	undique
arena	arena	from where	unde
around	circum	games	ludi
I become	fio	gift	donum
before	ante	slave girl	ancilla
I begin	coepi	gladiator	gladiator
I blame	vitupero	I go towards	adeo
building	aedificium	great	magnus
I call on	invoco	greatly	magnopere
calmly	placide	I grieve	doleo
candidate	candidatus	ground	humus
I carry	veho	guard	custos
charioteer	auriga	guest	hospes
citizen	civis	harbour	portus
clear	clarus	head	caput
client	cliens	heat	aestus
I close	claudo	here	hic
comrade	comes	home	sedes
consul	consul	hope	spes
conversation	sermo	I hope	spero
I count	numero	senate house	curia
countryside	rus	how	quomodo
course	cursus	husband	maritus
I cover	tego	ill	aeger
craftsman	faber	in fact	re
cup	poculum	inn	taberna
daily	cotidie	innkeeper	caupo
the next day	postridie	into	in
I decide	constituo	island	insula
delay	mora	judge	iudex
dictator	dictator	just as	sicut
dining room	triclinium	law	ius
dirty	sordidus	I learn	disco
doctor	medicus	leisure	otium
doorkeeper	ianitor	life	vita
I eject	eicio	lowly	humilis
enemy	inimicus	man	vir

poor man	pauper	spring	ver
young man	iuvenis	squared	quadratus
I meet	occurro	staff	baculum
merchant	mercator	steward	vilicus
mistress	domina	I stick	haereo
money	aes	stone	lapis
mother	mater	I stop	consisto
mouse	mus	I study	studeo
mud	lutum	sweet	dulcis
I offer	offero	table	tabella
only	modo	tear	lacrima
opinion	sententia	that	iste
palace	aula	the next day	postridie
parent	parens	them	eas
play	fabula	themselves	se
poor	egens	there	illuc
poor man	pauper	therefore	igitur
I prefer	malo	thick	densus
priest	sacerdos	thief	fur
queen	regina	thousand	mille
very quickly	celerrime	thus	ita
I raise	tollo	to	ad
recently	nuper	to him	ei
I recite	recito	to them	eis
I recover	recupero	to where	quo
I refuse	recuso	tomb	sepulcrum
I remove	removeo	too much	nimium
repeatedly	identidem	I go towards	adeo
rock	saxum	I treat	tracto
dining room	triclinium	treaty	foedus
I rush	ruo	truly	re vera
school	schola	very quickly	celerrime
sea	mare	I visit	viso
I seize	occupo	wall	murus
senate house	curia	war	bellum
senator	senator	way	via
series	ordo	we	nos
seven	septem	I weep	fleo
shoulder	umerus	what	quid
I sing	cano	from where	unde
I sing	canto	which	quod
sister	soror	white	candidus
slave	puer	without	sine
slave	servus	wolf	lupus
slave girl	ancilla	woman	mulier
I smell	olfacio	work	labor
I snore	sterto	worthy	dignus
so many	tot	year	annus
so that	ut	yes	ita vero
son	filius	young man	iuvenis
speaker	orator		
speech	oratio	(195 Latin words)	
speed	celeritas		

Word List 4

above	super	lance	lancea
I adore	adoro	I lead back	reduco
again	rursus	my	mea
I agree	consentio	nothing	nihil
always	semper	pig	sus
beautiful	pulcher	I put out	expono
before	antequam	savage	saevus
bird	avis	sheep	ovis
cat	feles	smell	odor
I collapse	concido	sparrow	passer
donkey	asinus	spine	spina
elephant	elephantus	status	dignitas
enough	satis	stitch	sutura
erase	erado	I take	sumo
estate	praedium	talker	orator
fish	piscis	thus	sic
for	enim	to be	esse
girlfriend	amica	treats	tractat
I indicate	indico	wife	uxor
joy	gaudium		
kitchen	culina	(38 Latin words)	

ALSO AVAILABLE
LATIN AND GREEK PUZZLE BOOKS

These collections are aimed at those who want to have some fun with the Latin and ancient Greek languages they know and love. All of these books feature solutions at the back, for those who get stuck.

Tricky Latin Puzzles raises the bar high for Latinists and is aimed at those who have studied the language for two or three years at least. The latest edition of the book boasts many revisions and improvements, so its 65 crossword puzzles, word-games and assorted brainteasers should bring plenty of fun.

Easy Greek Puzzles is a set of 60 brainteasers, improved and extended from the original edition, with 10 entirely new puzzles and accents incorporated for the first time. The book was first assembled from two short lists of words commonly used in a variety of beginners' courses and uses all five cases of noun, adjective and pronoun systems, as well as the active indicative verb endings from the present, imperfect, aorist and future tenses. It is appropriate for use by those who have studied the language for around one year or longer.

Tricky Greek Puzzles was written for those whose command of ancient Greek may allow them to enjoy its challenges - not for the faint-hearted. It includes 50 crosswords, sudokus, wordsearches and other brainteasers and is aimed at those who have studied the language for two or three years at least.

QUARE ID FACIAM

Nil nisi latinum, nil nisi quod Cicero ipse resolvere potuisset.

Centum ludi verbis latinis in hoc libro compositi sunt in quibus gaudium et quietem e tempestate invenire possis. Inter aenigmata sunt verba transversa, favi, sagittae, coniunctis quaerendis, numeratis numerandis, novomnia, verbomnia, hodierna latinata, verba instructa.

Centum aenigmata sunt in libro sed si diligentius respicias, fortasse unum insuper videas. Si hoc aenigma CI repertum confeceris, nomen tuum in nostrum album optimatium infra referetur.

"Si hoc intellegis...
Si lingua latina te delectat...
Si ludi cum verbis tibi oblectationem praebent...

Tibi hic liber est!"
Stephen Jenkin, The Classics Library

SONNETS FOR CLASSICAL STARS

This book was written as a follow-up companion to our earlier volume of poems, *Sonnets for Yorkshire Stars*. It contains 100 poems about leading figures in the ancient world, from the mythological to the historical, the literary to the artistic. The split in the book is roughly 50-50 Greek to Roman and the list of names included contains Poseidon, Homer, Nero and even Lesbia. The four main categories of the classical stars are Sagas and Stories, Sanctuaries and Shrines, Skill and Style and State and Standing. Highly recommended for the more poetic sort of classicist.

"Here are sonnets as history essays, as digests of the past, as mini encyclopedias and as rhyming invitations to explore further. So enjoy, and explore further!"
Ian McMillan

CLASSICAL PUZZLES

Classical Puzzles is a collection of brainteasers which focuses on the literature, culture and history of the ancient world rather than its languages. There are many people fascinated by classical civilisation who have not studied Latin and Greek and up until now, they may have been denied some fun: this book is an attempt to put that right and to complement our existing range of Latin and Greek puzzle books, not to mention the Yorkshire ones. This collection will test your knowledge of the Greeks and Romans with crosswords, sudokus and all kinds of wordgames to challenge you. Go on, test yourself out.

Can you separate your Caesars from your Ciceros? Your Spartans from your Athenians? It's all here: from art and architecture to geography, from politics to literature, from history to myths; a cornucopia of classical civilisation!

ROMAN BRITAIN PUZZLES

Britannia's the game

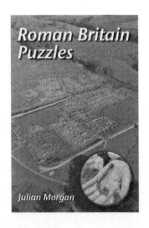

How well do you know Roman Britain? You'll soon find out, if you take on these 50 assorted crosswords and brainteasers. Caesar, Claudius and Hadrian all feature, as do sites from Vindolanda to Bignor, from Caerleon to Colchester. Roads, villas, artwork and inscriptions will test you to the max. Don't worry though - all the answers are in the back!

"These puzzles will provide great fun for the casual student of Roman Britain and will even challenge the experts in places."

Barbara Birley, The Vindolanda Trust

IMPERIUM LATIN COURSE

The Imperium Latin course has been written for the twenty-first century; unique, highly resourced and written to make fullest use of modern technology. Its texts follow the life of the Emperor Hadrian from his early childhood to his later years, as he became the most powerful man in the Roman world.

Imperium was released for general use in 2013, after a trialling period of six years. It consists of three course books, a Grammar and Syntax book, a puzzle book and the Imperium Latin Unseens collection for advanced users. All of these texts can be ordered through Amazon but are also available as pdf files in our Site Support Packs, which can be bought by schools. The three course books are also available as free of charge downloadable pdf files, from the TES Resources website.

"Much thought and effort has gone into keeping the course rigorous and quick-paced, without overwhelming or discouraging students. The amount of assistance and supplemental material available to teachers as they present this course is truly remarkable."

Sharon Kazmierski, Classical Outlook, Fall 2013

A SERIES OF YORKSHIRE PUZZLES

  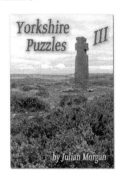

There are three books in the Yorkshire Puzzles series. Each one boasts 50 puzzles, including crosswords and other types of word-games written to test your knowledge of the county. Don't expect to find them easy unless you are an expert on Yorkshire dialect, cricket, brass bands, geography, history... and so the list goes on.

What they said about the first book in the series:

"Aimed at the more knowledgeable reader, this volume is filled with tough questions that will challenge even the most ardent Yorkshirephiles."

Dalesman, February 2017

SONNETS FOR YORKSHIRE STARS

The poems in this collection have been written to celebrate 100 of the county's outstanding achievers. The list of their names was compiled carefully to reflect all aspects of life, so you'll find artists, musicians, politicians, sporting personalities and writers here: Yorkshire's finest, all celebrated in fourteen-line verse.

"So honoured that you chose to write of me and am delighted it was in the form of a poem and not a puzzle! Warmest good wishes."

Baroness Betty Boothroyd

"I feel flattered to be portrayed in verse."

Peter Wright, The Yorkshire Vet

"Many thanks. Very interesting to read about my fellow Yorkshire folk."

Dickie Bird

"perfectly crafted stories that brim with rhythm and dance with rhyme."

Ian McMillan

WORLD OF JAMES HERRIOT PUZZLES

Fans of the world's most famous vet, pencils at the ready! This collection was made in collaboration with the World of James Herriot in Thirsk and includes 50 puzzles, based on all eight books of the famous vet's memoirs as well as on-screen depictions, including the BBC series *All creatures great and small*.

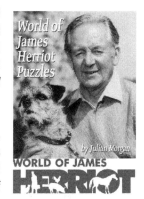

Animals and ailments, colleagues and customers, potions and powders of the original books of memoirs are all here, as well as on-screen portrayals of vets and locations, both real and fictional. Don't worry though. If it all gets too much, the solutions are in the back.

"This volume of puzzles comes from the pen of Yorkshire Author Julian Morgan and closely matches the content of the books written by James Herriot. The challenges posed vary from simple wordsearch to cryptic conundrum and will surely appeal to Herriot fans of all ages. Julian's puzzles are respectful in adhering to the original stories and will bring new ways for readers to connect again with the stories they love."

Ian Ashton, Managing Director, World of James Herriot

CITY OF YORK PUZZLES

This collection will provide hours of amusement for fans of our great county town, boasting 50 assorted crosswords and challenging word-games of various types. Facets of history, arts, attractions, streets, famous faces, sports, pubs and shops all feature, so if you love York, you should love what's on offer here.

Not for the faint-hearted, it's a good job you can find the answers in the back. So go on, how well do you know York?

ABOUT THE AUTHOR

Julian Morgan served as a teacher and a Head of Classics for many years in the UK and in Germany. Julian has now stepped down from classroom teaching and is very happy to be living in his native Yorkshire once again.

Julian has written a wide range of educational software titles and books in the last 35 years, publishing many of these under the banner of his business, J-PROGS. His Imperium Latin course is used in a good number of schools and can be downloaded free of charge by following the links from www.imperiumlatin.com.

He can often be found walking his dog in the Great Wold Valley of North Yorkshire, where he lives.

To find out more, see www.j-progs.com

Twitter feed: @imperiumlatin

Printed in Great Britain
by Amazon

57845459R00059